Trans Pleasure

Trans Pleasure

ON GENDER LIBERATION AND
SEXUAL FREEDOM

Brandon Andrew Robinson

 UNIVERSITY OF CALIFORNIA PRESS

University of California Press
Oakland, California

© 2026 by Brandon Andrew Robinson

All rights reserved.

Names: Robinson, Brandon Andrew, author.
Title: Trans pleasure : on gender liberation and sexual freedom / Brandon Andrew Robinson.
Description: Oakland, California : University of California Press, [2026] | Includes bibliographical references and index.
Identifiers: LCCN 2025032641 (print) | LCCN 2025032642 (ebook) | ISBN 9780520410329 (cloth) | ISBN 9780520410336 (paperback) | ISBN 9780520410343 (ebook)
Subjects: LCSH: Transgender women—Sexual behavior. | Lesbians—Sexual behavior.
Classification: LCC HQ77.94.S48 R63 2026 (print) | LCC HQ77.94.S48 (ebook)
LC record available at https://lccn.loc.gov/2025032641
LC ebook record available at https://lccn.loc.gov/2025032642

GPSR Authorized Representative: Easy Access System Europe, Mustamäe tee 50, 10621 Tallinn, Estonia, gpsr.requests@easproject.com

35 34 33 32 31 30 29 28 27 26
10 9 8 7 6 5 4 3 2 1

To a more pleasurable tomorrow

Contents

Acknowledgments ix

1. Compulsory Heterosexuality and the Trans Femme Existence 1
2. Sexual Cissexism 19
3. Comfort and the Paradox of Pleasure 47
4. t4t possibilities 72
5. Gender Liberation and the Abolition of Sexual Identities 98

   Methodological Appendix A. t4t as Methods 125
   Methodological Appendix B. Interview Guide 135
   Notes 139
   References 149
   Index 165

Acknowledgments

I've always found pleasure in reading acknowledgment sections of academic books. For some reason, people—including authors themselves—often think of writing as a lonely and isolating endeavor. Acknowledgment sections, though, have always challenged that solitary writer idea for me, as these sections often reveal the pleasurable relations and beautiful communities that authors engage with while writing their book. The same is true for myself. I was and am so fortunate to be in conversation and in community with so many brilliant, inspiring people. These folks have all brought pleasure, joy, and meaning to my life. And I am so thankful for each and every one of them. These acknowledgments cannot even begin to express my gratitude.

First and foremost, I am thankful to my main writing group—Anima Adjepong and Shameka Powell. We formed our group in 2018. And they are the only people to have read and provided feedback on every chapter of this book *and* on my last book. They truly exemplify the ethics and care of trans for trans (t4t) relations. The love and attentiveness that they give to my writing is invaluable. They push me to expand my thinking and myself. And they always excite me to want to return to my writing. Thank you both from the bottom of my heart for all the pleasurable years of critical engagement. I look forward to many more together.

I am also thankful for my University of California, Riverside (UCR) writing group—Crystal Mun-hye Baik, Victoria Reyes, Jade Sasser, and Randol Contreras. A great deal of their feedback on earlier articles and drafts helped to shape the ideas that came to be chapter 2 of this book. I feel so lucky to work alongside of so many cutting-edge scholars at UCR. And it was a joy to get to workshop our ideas and research with one another. I'm excited about the great things we will continue to do at our university.

Speaking of UCR, I am beyond grateful for being in the most supportive and loving department. My colleagues are truly badass feminists, who deeply care about making this world a better place. They push me to want to be a better academic, a better educator, and a better person. I am inspired by them all. Thank you to Crystal Mun-hye Baik, Jack Cáraves, Katja Guenther, Sherine Hafez, Tammy Ho, Victoria Reyes, Liz Rubio, and Jade Sasser. It is truly an honor to think, write, and teach alongside all of you. Jane Ward, your presence is missed in this department, and I thank you for all the conversations and all the pleasurable times together. Thank you as well to so many staff members at UCR, especially the Gender and Sexuality Studies (GSST) staff—Diana Marroquin, Irene Dotson, and Angela Cherry. I do not know how I could have chaired this department without all of you. Thank you for being the backbone of this university and for all your labor and love.

To the students at UCR—especially the GSST students—you galvanize me. Indeed, some ideas in this book began as discussions in the classroom, whereby UCR students brilliantly and incisively questioned some classic texts that we read. I am in awe of how UCR students constantly show up, and they always remind me how magical learning and the classroom can be. Thank you for keeping the enchantment alive.

A special thank you—always—to Salvador Vidal-Ortiz. I appreciate you beyond words. Thank you for the walks, the texts, the voice memos, and for the love. You have made me the scholar I am today. And I deeply value our friendship. Thank you as well to Angela Jones for always being the best. I find so much pleasure in every moment we spend together. And I wish the entire world for you.

While working on this book, I was also working on another project—the Family, Housing, and Me (FHAM) Project. To Amy L. Stone, you have breathed new life into my mid-career, and you are the best collaborator I could ever ask for. I adore you, and I am so excited for what is to come next. Thank you, as well, to the core FHAM team of Javania Michelle Webb, Otis McCandless-Chapman, and Chiara Pride. I loved our weekly meetings and group chats. It was a pleasure conducting FHAM with all of you. And it is a joy to collaborate during these trying times. Thank you also to all the undergraduate research assistants on FHAM. Your work was invaluable and allowed me to focus on writing this book while also collecting data for the next book.

For this project, thank you to my research team—Kori Pacyniak, Shell Morales, Laura Rodriguez Pinto, and Stephanie Gutierrez. Y'all helped to make me a better mentor and person. I appreciate all the labor that you have given to this work. Your care, your love, your sharp interviewing skills, and your passion—all made this project and book what it is. Thank you.

To Naomi Schneider, thank you for always believing in my work and supporting my ideas. Also at UC Press, thank you to Aline Dolinh. To my developmental editor—Beth Sherouse at The Outside Reader—you are magic. Thank you for all the feedback and line-by-line edits and for the care you gave to the stories in this book and to keeping my voice. You really made this book shine. Thank you, as well, to Ben Alexander for copyediting this book. And thank you to Ideas on Fire for indexing this book. Thank you also to Carla Pfeffer, Angela Jones, Cati Connell, and Chris Barcelos who reviewed this manuscript at different stages and provided the most incisive, supportive feedback any scholar could ask for. This book is better because of you.

Thanks to my friends for putting up with me. Kristin Sosa, you are my day one. I love you. Thank you to Chrissy Moses, Gerry Gorospe, and Kevin McKinnon—you have made life in LA a dream. Shantel Buggs, our friendship has changed me for good. Thank you as well to my fit fam—Melissa Widjaja, Olivia Richman, and Gabby Pajo—you have made working out fun (if that is possible), and I always look forward to suffering with you. Thank you to Haus of Meeshie—Michelle Fahmy—and to Hayley Yerington for designing and turning my home into the most glorious deconstructed rainbow. My sanctuary now brings me so much pleasure, and it was a joy to write this book in such a vibrant, creative space. Thank you as well to Yola Hernandez for keeping my home beautiful and clean.

Part of chapter 2 was previously published as "Transamorous Misogyny: Masculinity, Heterosexuality, and Cis Men's Sexist Desires for Trans Women" in *Men & Masculinities* 26(3): 356–75. Another part of chapter 2 was previously published as "Super Straights: Heterosexuality, White Supremacy, and Transphobia Without Transphobes" in *Bulletin of Applied Transgender Studies* 3(1–2): 137–57. And some ideas from chapters 3 and 4 were published as "'I Feel the Most Pleasure When I Don't Have to Worry': On Sexual Comfort, t4t, and Trans Pleasure" in *Sex & Sexualities* 1(1): 18–24.

Lastly, thank you to the trans women and femmes who were interviewed for this study. Thank you for sharing the full complexities of your dating and sexual experiences. Your words and lives matter. Your pleasure matters. You matter. And because of all of you and your willingness to share your life stories, may we get to a better, more pleasurable tomorrow.

1   Compulsory Heterosexuality and the Trans Femme Existence

"I try to use my platform to let people know that I'm not straight and that doesn't take away from my womanhood," said 26-year-old Imani, who got on Zoom to be interviewed about trans women's and femmes' dating and sexual experiences.[1] Living in Greensboro, North Carolina, and working in food service as a floater, Imani went on to discuss how the experience of being a bisexual trans woman challenges prevailing ideas about gender and sexuality. As Imani explained, "Sometimes I feel like, 'Oh, this is kinda cringy if I talk about not being straight all the time.' But then it's the only reason why I'm doing this is because people genuinely don't feel trans women can be anything but straight, and they'll be like, 'Oh, what's the point of being trans if you're just gonna date women?'" Imani explicitly understood that ideas about heterosexuality are tied to dominant ideas about gender. "A lot of people perform gender specifically for the other sex and not for themselves," Imani delineated. "So, I feel when you have someone like me who doesn't perform for the opposite sex, it's kind of a shock to people."

It may come as a surprise to some, but many trans women and femmes are "anything but straight," as Imani stated. In simplistic terms, gender identity is someone's internal and individual self-conception about being a man, woman, nonbinary, or another gender. Sexual orientation is someone's internal and individual self-conception about their emotional, romantic, and sexual attractions—of being gay, straight, lesbian, bisexual, or another sexual identity. In a society that privileges heterosexuality, people often assume women, including trans women, are straight and desire men.[2] But like Imani, many trans women and femmes don't exclusively want or desire cishet men.[3] Despite prevalent assumptions about trans people, gender identity does not dictate sexual orientation—and trans people are not all heterosexuals.

Indeed, only three of the forty-eight trans women and femmes interviewed for this study identified as straight or heterosexual (and one of those three identified as "straight, tragically"). Many identified as queer, pansexual, bisexual, asexual, or another identity that eschews the gender binary (and genitals) as how to conceptualize their desires and attractions. In general, trans folks are more likely to not identify as heterosexual compared to cis folks.[4] Studies have shown that over two-thirds of trans people identify as bisexual, queer, or something other than heterosexual or homosexual.[5] Trans people are more likely to indicate an attraction to more than one gender. And trans people may be more likely to question how sexual identity often centers on binary notions of gender. In other words, identities such as heterosexual often privilege gender—and mainly genitals—as the best way to think about, define, and organize sexual attraction. In turn, dominant understandings of sexual identities often reify notions of gender essentialism—the idea that gender is fixed and determined by biology—and often reify notions of the gender binary—the idea that men and women are the only genders.[6] Trans people have historically complicated and challenged these simplistic notions of gender, sexuality, and identity and continue to do so.

But despite Imani's questioning of dominant ways of thinking about gender and sexuality, Imani's statement still shows the power of heterosexuality. To be a "proper" woman in U.S. society is to be straight.[7] To perform femininity appropriately is to desire and date men. Dominant ideas of gender are in many ways dependent on heterosexuality. And trans folks are caught up in these ideas about gender and sexuality as well. Historically, medical doctors, psychologists, and other professional gatekeepers—all mainly cis men—would often only allow trans women access to gender-affirming care if they said they were heterosexual and if they planned to date and marry a cishet man.[8] Trans people who did not report a heterosexual identity were often denied access to affirming care.[9] Imagining trans people partnering with other trans people, or imagining lesbian, bisexual, pansexual, and queer trans people seemed impossible or deviant for these gatekeepers. In erasing queer trans people, these gatekeepers kept heterosexuality as the norm.

But recent increases in trans visibility, especially through social media, have allowed some trans people today to imagine life and relationships beyond heterosexuality and the gender binary. As Imani detailed, "And then once I started to watch more YouTube videos about lesbian trans women—just literally typing it into YouTube, 'lesbian trans women' or 'bisexual trans women'—I started to see, you can be a trans woman and not be straight. You can be a trans woman and not be focused on men and not present as feminine." Imani continued, "Basically, it started to help me realize that femininity isn't to the service of men, and specifically to serve cishet men. And femininity is for yourself. And the purpose of womanhood is not to serve men."

Imani found expansive ideas about gender and sexuality through social media created by and centering trans people. This medium can allow trans people (or anyone really) to learn about and challenge dominant notions of sex, gender, and sexuality.[10] Importantly, trans social media is not produced by a cis majority, and cis people are often not the target audience.[11] Trans social media is often trans for trans (t4t)—meaning by trans people and for trans people—and can thus disrupt culturally dominant (i.e., cis) ways of thinking about gender and sexuality. This trans representation also expands gender and femininity away from a focus on cis desires and heterosexuality. It challenges the idea that heterosexuality defines womanhood and that femininity should be in service to men. For Imani, femininity can be about enjoying oneself and one's own gender, sexuality, and embodiment rather than about pleasing others. This type of t4t content expanded Imani's ideas of gender and sexuality and presents broad possibilities beyond compulsory heterosexuality.

A Trans Twist with Adrienne Rich

As the title of this chapter suggests, this book draws on feminist Adrienne Rich's 1980 essay "Compulsory Heterosexuality and the Lesbian Existence," wherein Rich argued that heterosexuality is a *political institution* that is imposed, managed, organized, propagandized, and maintained by force.[12] Heterosexuality may feel innate or freely chosen. But through overt social forces, such as physical violence, and through covert ideological processes, such as erasing the existence of lesbians or constructing lesbians as deviant and immoral, women are often forced into heterosexuality. Moreover, as Rich contended, this institution—heterosexuality—often deeply harms, hurts, and exploits women. Indeed, women often feel unsatisfied, disappointed, and entrapped in relationships with men. Women deal with sexual harassment from men.[13] And women navigate the constant misogyny wherein men devalue women and femininity (while supposedly also desiring women).[14] Heterosexuality, then, upholds the patriarchy and gender inequality, largely by maintaining men's power through men's physical, economic, and emotional access to women.[15] And yet, many feminists still fail to question how compulsory heterosexuality harms women.

This book returns to Rich's concept of compulsory heterosexuality and exposes how it harms trans women and femmes. I ask: How does compulsory heterosexuality shape the experiences of trans women and femmes and their dating and sex lives? Moreover, how can trans desires, trans pleasure, and trans relationships challenge and disrupt this oppressive institution? In exploring these questions, I chart new paths in dismantling compulsory heterosexuality and in moving toward gender liberation.

Notably, these questions arose both from my own engagement with Rich's classic work and from conversations with my students, who are coming of age in a time of much wider visibility and dialogue about gender and trans people. Indeed, the first time I ever taught Rich's piece at the University of California, Riverside, several students critiqued the essay for being gender essentialist, especially Rich's notion of the lesbian experience being a "profoundly *female* experience."[16] Students wondered if and how trans people could fit into Rich's theorizing. I mean, there are trans lesbians. There are folks like Imani. So, partly thanks to my brilliant students, I return to the concept but with a trans twist.

This twist involves interrogating heterosexuality as a prime mechanism of maintaining cisness—the idea that gender and sex are binary and biological truths. As sociologist alithia zamantakis astutely defines it, cisness is "a political, discursive, and social manifestation that creates a misunderstanding of reality as naturally and binarily gendered and sexed and of trans people as deviant and/or pathological."[17] Importantly, heterosexuality implies cisness, as heterosexuality relies on and erotizes the gender binary.[18] And while categories such as bisexual and pansexual have troubled the hetero/homo binary, heterosexuality still structures how many people often think about and experience sex, gender, and sexuality. But, as I will show, in maintaining the gender binary, compulsory heterosexuality (and its link to cisness) harms trans people. And part of what makes transness so threatening to the status quo is how transness disrupts dominant notions of sex, gender, and sexuality. That is, a main component of the modern backlash toward trans people is the fact that transness challenges these often taken for granted categories of embodiment, identity, and desire. But compulsory heterosexuality (along with its concurrent sexual labels) limits our desires and imaginations. It limits how we can love and feel pleasure. We must imagine different ways of being in this world if we are all going to get free.

To the Bedroom

In this book, I explore the lives of trans people outside of the doctor's office, the workplace, the family, and social movements—the contexts in which trans people have received the most attention from sociologists and from other social science scholars.[19] Instead, I turn to the bedroom, to the park, to restaurants, to dating apps, to Reddit, and to other spaces and places that capture the everyday dating and sex lives of trans women and femmes. If we want to understand social change, we can look to dating and sex, as dating and sex can often tell us a great deal about how a social group experiences the broader society.[20] Indeed, a narrative often told to trans people to try to discourage transition is that they will never experience love or find anyone to love them.[21] And while this book will document instances of discrimination (as discrimination is, unfortunately, part of the complexities and fullness of trans people's lives), this book also moves away from just focusing on violence toward trans people and their construction as "vulnerable subjects."[22] Instead, this book examines trans people as both desiring and desirable subjects.

Notably, this book is about trans women and femmes. This book is not about all trans people. I assume that many of the experiences and dynamics detailed in this book—navigating dating and hooking up, and negotiating sex, gender, sexuality, and desire—look different for trans men and trans masculine folks compared to trans women and femmes. My hope is for future scholarship to continue exploring the dating and sex lives of all trans people, including trans men and trans masculine people, especially as we work to capture the fullness of trans lives and trans experiences.

The primary source material for this book is 48 qualitative interviews conducted with trans women and trans femmes in the fall of 2022. All interviewees are from the United States and over half are trans women and femmes of color. I examine their dating, hookup, and sex lives to explore how heterosexuality, sexual identities, and the gender binary structure our desires. I also explore the pleasurable possibilities of reimagining how we can experience gender, sexuality, and desire outside of these oppressive institutions and labels.

To be clear, queer theory has long shown how our sexual desires, behaviors, and identities do not neatly align.[23] In this book, however, I focus in on how compulsory heterosexuality hurts and marginalizes trans people. For instance, transness blurs the borders of heterosexuality and destabilizes notions of sexual orientation, which often privileges gender and genitalia.[24] Transness can make us question our desires, question the gender binary, and even question our notions of heterosexuality and homosexuality—identities we often think are so innate to who we are. In turn, violence against trans people can be a way to try to reinforce dominant ideas of the gender binary and heterosexuality.[25] By centering, then, the dating and sex lives of trans women and trans femmes, I document how compulsory heterosexuality and sexual identities thwart pleasure and subjugate trans people. Ultimately, compulsory heterosexuality obstructs our path to gender liberation. It limits how we experience pleasure, love, and relationships. And we must question and challenge it. Therefore, this book also documents how trans women and femmes resist oppression and the political institution that is heterosexuality. In documenting this resistance, this book centers trans pleasures and trans desires in order to theorize other possibilities—pleasurable possibilities—of achieving gender liberation and sexual freedom.

Dating, Hooking Up, and the Trans Femme Experience

The remaining chapters of this book turn to the dating, hookup, and sex lives of trans women and femmes to examine the lived experiences and material realities of how the gender binary and heterosexuality shape trans lives. In doing so, it documents the harms created by compulsory heterosexuality and cisness. But it also documents trans pleasures and trans desires that challenge these structures of oppression. Let's return to Imani to get a glimpse of what this book is about.

Sexual Cissexism: Fetishization and Hypersexualization

"I'd assume most of the guys I've had sex with probably fetishized trans women. And that's kind of just is what it is," stated Imani, who was single during the time of the study. "Straight guys usually are really attracted to me. But again, because I've had so many lackluster experiences with guys, I don't really date that many guys anymore. And I don't really consider them to be in my dating or hooking-up pool." On hookup apps such as Grindr, Imani saw many men as "chasers," who would fetishize trans women as "crossdressers or hyper-feminine men." In response, Imani stopped using Grindr and other similar apps. "I don't use Grindr at all now," Imani explained.

As chapter 2 will discuss, part of how cisness and heterosexuality remain as norms is through fetishizing trans women. Trans women often have to be *hyper*feminine and *hyper*sexual in order to be seen and desired as women.[26] Cis women are the norm to which trans women get compared—a process that delegitimizes trans women's womanhood as they are only accepted as women in comparison to cis women. People may also see trans women as just hyperfeminine men, again delegitimizing their womanhood. And these experiences echoed frequently in the interviews with the trans women and femmes in this study, many of whom have had lackluster experiences with straight men and were tired of dealing with being fetishized. Imani partly resists this fetishization by not really dating or hooking up with cishet guys anymore and by not using hookup apps anymore. But this resistance can limit Imani's dating and sex options and the spaces and places where Imani can meet people for dates and sexual encounters. That is, Imani's experiences reflect how, in a society still dominated by compulsory heterosexuality, trans women are often positioned as nonnormative—as hyperfeminine and hypersexual—in a way that constrains their choices and limits their relationships.

These dynamics can be even more complicated for trans women and femmes of color. As Imani explained, "Firstly, I'm a Black woman. Hard stop. My experiences—how people interact with me, how I interact with people—are largely defined by me being a Black woman and how Black womanhood is perceived in America. Then after that, I'm a Black trans woman and that's a whole other set of experiences." Gender, including being trans, intersects with other social categories such as race, whereby experiences of sexism, racism, *and* transphobia can produce what sociologist Patricia Hill Collins calls "intersecting oppressions."[27] And these intersections create unique lived experiences for Black trans women.

In 1851, formerly enslaved abolitionist and activist Sojourner Truth purportedly asked the audience at a Women's Rights Convention in Ohio, "Ain't I a Woman?" In delivering this speech, Truth evoked the numerous ways that Black women experienced womanhood differently than white women. Under slavery, Black women worked, plowed, and had to "bear the lash" just like enslaved men. Black women were not "helped into carriages" or "lifted over ditches" like white women.[28] U.S. society desexualized certain Black women as "mammies" or hypersexualized them as "jezebels," while constructing white womanhood as demure, modest, and physically weak and in need of white male protection.[29] White womanhood was partially constructed in contradistinction to these racist controlling images of Black women. These interlocking racial and gender dynamics of antebellum society subjected Black women to sexual abuse and forced childbirth and denied enslaved Black men the patriarchal roles of protectors and providers.[30] Through slavery, then, Black people were ungendered, and Black women were positioned outside of proper womanhood.[31] These dynamics have remained prevalent even as slavery was replaced by Jim Crow, lynching, convict leasing, and mass incarceration in the modern era. Today, Black women still experience gender differently than white women (and women of other races). Black women are often seen as more masculine and aggressive compared to white women, and stereotypes of the desexualized "mammy" and hypersexual "jezebel" too often still prevail.[32] Black trans women like Imani, then, have to deal with the hypersexualization of Black women and the hypersexualization of trans women.[33] Racial fetishization intersects with trans fetishization to make navigating the dating and hooking-up landscape even more difficult for Black trans women and femmes.

The next chapter further explores my theory of how sexuality (including sexual identities and sexual desires) often maintains cisness and subjugates trans people—a concept I call *sexual cissexism*. Like Imani's story, chapter 2 shows how sexual stereotypes about trans people, such as trans women being hypersexual, lead to discrimination toward trans folks and how these stereotypes keep heterosexuality and cisness as the desired norms within U.S. society. Chapter 2 also explores how sexual cissexism intersects with sexual racism to harm trans women and femmes of color in particular ways. Ultimately, sexual cissexism, sexual racism, and sexual stereotypes harm and limit trans women's and femmes' lives.

Comfort: Stripping Sexual Stereotypes

Beyond dating and the apps, dominant ideas about gender and sexuality shape actual sexual experiences as well. "A lot of times when I hook up with guys, it's more of they wanna come over, and have sex, leave. They're very disconnected from the experience," Imani explained. "When I would hook up with a girl, we're hanging out. It's more of an intimate type of situation." Gender stereotypes shape sexual encounters. As Imani further elaborated, "Sometimes with girls, it's kinda like, 'Oh, do you use your genitals?' Or like, 'How do you like have sex?' And I just tell them, 'Yeah, I'm cool with that. I'm cool topping.' And the guys, they usually automatically assume that I want to be penetrated. So, they don't usually ask that many questions."

Cis ideas about gender, sex, and heterosexuality can shape people's sexual experiences, including trans people's sexual encounters. In Imani's experience, men often want to just fuck, but women seek intimacy—desires that strongly reflect dominant ideas of gender and heterosexuality.[34] Women often want Imani to top or penetrate them—an act associated with the dominant masculine role in a sexual relationship—and men assume Imani wants to be penetrated—a role associated with womanhood and submissiveness.[35] In other words, dominant gender scripts about topping, bottoming, and intimacy can shape the sexual landscape that trans women and femmes have to navigate. For trans women and femmes of color, they may also have to navigate the racialized sexual stereotypes of people of color, which often construct Black people as dominant and hypersexual, Asian people as submissive, and Latinx people as exotic.[36] Stereotypes can shape sexual experiences.

But comfort can be an antidote. In recalling a date that went well, Imani talked about going to a bar arcade with a trans guy where they played a lot of Japanese games, as Imani likes anime. They also had fun playing Dance Dance Revolution. In discussing why this date with another trans person went well, Imani said, "Just feeling comfortable being around someone and just being able to be myself, and not really worrying about what else was going on around me was the most fun part."

Chapter 3 explores the concept of comfort, including sexual comfort, to show how it can be a foundational mode of experiencing fun and pleasure, especially pleasure that challenges cisness and compulsory heterosexuality. Comfort can allow people to find respect and fulfillment in just being themselves. It can allow for dating and sexual experiences outside of the harms of sexual stereotypes. Comfort can point us toward how to care for and connect with one another, and it can teach us how to relate differently to one another through consent and communication. Comfort can offer us a path to gender liberation.

t4t: Beyond Heterosexuality

t4t might offer us a path as well. Indeed, many of the trans folks in this study have often dated other trans people. As Imani explained, "I usually date women, other trans women, other nonbinary people, or trans men. They're typically also usually Black." In addition to the comfort Imani found on the arcade date with the trans guy, Imani discussed another recent date with a nonbinary person that also went well. "So, they came to Greensboro, and we were supposed to go to the art museum, but the art museum was closed, and I didn't realize that when I suggested we go there," Imani recalled.

"So, we ended up going downtown to the bar, and we just hung out downtown during the day and took pictures and went to a cool vintage shop and went to the bar and just kind of hung out." This date was the type Imani prefers. "It wasn't a formal 'Let's go somewhere specific.' It was more of a 'Let's just hang out' type of date, which is more of what I prefer. Because I like to do a lot of stuff and I kind of get sidetracked by things easily. So, I like to just go from places and kinda explore." On this t4t date, Imani could just hang out, explore, and enjoy being with the other person without needing cis validation, without having to educate cis people about trans folks, and without worrying about being sexualized and stereotyped.

Notably, trans womanhood is often constructed as needing cis heterosexual validation—trans women need to be in a relationship with a cishet man to achieve womanhood.[37] Society maintains this cis heterosexual illusion partly through obscuring lesbian, bisexual, and other queer trans women. And it partly maintains this illusion through erasing t4t relationships, wherein trans people neither seek nor need cis people or their validation. Indeed, Imani and many others in this study did turn to t4t, which can offer space for eschewing cisness and everything it brings with it. In challenging the need for cis validation, t4t can also open up new dating and sexual scripts that don't rely on cisgender ideas of how to have sex or go on a date.[38] t4t can provide a respite for trans people trying to avoid being objectified and fetishized, allowing trans people to just enjoy a date with each other as people with shared interests. It can be a tactic for challenging cisness and compulsory heterosexuality.

In chapter 4, I propose that t4t can teach us strategies for achieving freedom and liberation. t4t can teach us about dismantling cis stereotypes. It can teach us about care, community, and connection.

And it can teach us about new modes of relating to one another. But t4t—especially as a separatist practice that privileges trans identity over other identities and experiences—cannot be the singular utopic end goal. t4t is complicated and ultimately limited. As Imani noted, Imani also prefers other Black people, which reveals how other social categories such as race can also shape dating and sexual connections. t4t, then, might have a "whiteness problem," as does much of the broader LGBTQ community, and t4t might overlook race and other social categories such as ability and religion in its sole focus on gender. Chapter 4 explores these possibilities and pitfalls of t4t. It teaches us what we should take from t4t but also exposes its limitations of being a separatist identity strategy that privileges trans identity over other identities and experiences.

The Ocean

On January 24, 2021, while I was eagerly waiting for the second season of *Euphoria*, I settled in to watch the special episode "Fuck Anyone Who's Not a Sea Blob." The entire episode focused on Jules—a trans character in therapy. While watching the episode, I couldn't believe what I was seeing. Did Jules really just say that to her therapist?

"I feel like I've framed my entire womanhood around men. When, like, in reality, I'm no longer interested in men," said Jules. "Like, philosophically. Like, like, what men want. Like, what men want is so boring. And simple, and not creative." Jules went on: "I just, like, I look at myself, and I'm like, how the fuck did I spend my entire life building this. Like . . . Like, my body, and my personality, and like, my soul around what I think men desire? It's just, like . . . it's embarrassing. I feel like a . . . a fraud."

The character Jules is played by trans actress Hunter Schafer, a white, skinny, blonde, conventionally attractive woman. During the beginning of *Euphoria*, Jules—a high school student at the time—is sleeping with an older white married man, a predator whom she meets on a hookup app. But eventually Jules starts dating Rue, a character played by Black actress Zendaya. As Jules starts dating Rue, Jules's ideas around womanhood and femininity shift. Indeed, Jules uses the word *fraud* to discuss how she felt about constructing her womanhood around men's desires—around heterosexual desires and dominant notions of white femininity. Jules's use of *fraud* flips the concept on its head. Often, trans women are constructed as deceivers, as not real women, as frauds.[39] For Jules, though, the fraudulent act is constructing femininity and womanhood in service to cis men's desires, in service to cis heterosexuality. Jules's revelation to the therapist evokes how heterosexuality limits and confines gender. It maintains cis understandings of the gender binary. It is boring, simple, not creative. It's embarrassing.

But outside of heterosexuality, gender can expand. "Femininity would always be this just, like, this, like elusive, distant thing, you know? Like unreachable," Jules explains. "But, uh, but then, I think about beautiful things that are also broad and deep, and thick, and I think of . . . something like the ocean. I think, like . . . that I want to be as beautiful as the ocean. 'Cause the ocean's strong as fuck. And feminine as fuck. And, like, both are what makes the ocean, the ocean."

Notably, Schafer cowrote the episode. And like Imani's story, this therapy session speaks to how notions of womanhood and femininity shift when they move away from appealing to cishet men, to heterosexuality. The ocean comes to represent this expansiveness of gender, which encompasses broadness, deepness, thickness, and strength within femininity's reach. The simile of the ocean can work to reconfigure something such as broad shoulders or a deep voice as "feminine as fuck." It is what makes the ocean the ocean. It is what makes a trans woman a woman. And it can expand our own thinking about gender and sexuality. As Imani explained, "Like Jules in *Euphoria*, I feel like she's probably the best representation in pop culture that is easily accessible to most people." Going on, Imani elaborated, "And seeing her kind of opened my eyes to the fact that trans women can kind of just be whatever. And like, your sexuality doesn't define your womanhood. And [this representation] really started to help me realize, 'Oh, someone can be trans and not be straight.'"

What, then, are the possibilities of gender—of freedom—outside of heterosexuality? In thinking through this question, especially in the last chapter, this book centers trans pleasures and trans desires in order to expand our thinking about gender and freedom beyond compulsory heterosexuality and beyond cisness. As this book will show, we must deal with how compulsory heterosexuality and cisness limit and constrain not only our experiences of sexuality and pleasure, but also our gender possibilities. That is, heterosexuality—as a political institution—maintains cisness. Gender liberation, then, will require its destruction.

Ultimately then, the time has come to think about trans pleasures and trans desires. Compulsory heterosexuality is thwarting pleasure. And if pleasure is a measure of freedom—that is, all people deserve pleasure, satisfaction, and fulfillment that is life-enriching[40]—then compulsory heterosexuality is a roadblock to gender liberation. We need new ways of yearning and desiring outside of compulsory heterosexuality and its concurrent sexual labels that limit our possibilities. Another world—a better, freer world—is possible. These things are what I dream of and yearn for. I teach these things. I believe in these things. And I write about these things. My hope, then, is for this book to get us one step closer to another life—a more pleasurable life—a life of sexual freedom and gender liberation for all.

2 *Sexual Cissexism*

"It's a nice feeling to be desired, but for the right reason. So, it's not like in a fetishize-y, hypersexualizing lens. But it feels great," stated 28-year-old Gabrielle, an administrative assistant for a college mentoring program in Gainesville, Florida. Gabrielle went on to discuss how trans women and femmes often experience a "hypersexualization-desexualization paradox."[1] As Gabrielle explained, "I'm hypersexualized, or I'm just desexualized altogether. But I'm not usually kind of fully seen as a fully developed person, I think because of my transness and how they perceive it to be." Gabrielle's experience echoes through many of the stories in this book. Through sexual objectification, trans women are often hypersexualized.[2] Folks may view trans women and femmes as hypersubmissive, hyperfeminine nymphos who are slutty, kinky, and always wanting sex.[3] Some people may view trans women and femmes as sexual objects who exist to fulfill other people's desires, rather than seeing trans women and femmes as full sexual or romantic partners with their own sexual desires and emotional needs. Or, through sexual rejection, people may view trans people as wholly undesirable, desexualized, and not even considered as a potential romantic or sexual partner.[4] Trans people are rarely desired or seen as just people.

This chapter is about what I term *sexual cissexism*—about how desire, including sexual desire, often maintains cisness and compulsory heterosexuality. It is partly a chapter about how even desires for trans people can maintain cisness. For instance, the hypersexualization of trans women and femmes positions trans women and femmes as outside of the desired norm, as they must be *hyper*feminine and *hyper*submissive in order to be desired. Trans women must be exceptional to be desired. Or they are desexualized and not desired at all. Through these processes, desire maintains cisness and heterosexuality as the dominant structures within society, as cisness and heterosexuality are the unmarked desired norms to which trans women and femmes are judged, evaluated, and compared to. In maintaining cisness and heterosexuality as the norms, sexual cissexism harms trans women and femmes as they must navigate these stereotypes and wholesale rejection within their dating and sex lives. Sexual cissexism also denies trans women and femmes their own pleasure, their own right to be fulfilled in relationships, and their own right to feel safe, loved, and desired in their own bodies. It denies trans women and femmes for who they are—fully developed people.

What Is Sexual Cissexism?

In the simplest terms, sexual cissexism is about how sexual identities, sexual practices, and sexual desires maintain cisness—that is, ideas about sexuality often reflect and reinforce dominant cis ideas about what our bodies, behaviors, and relationships should look like for others to consider us attractive and desirable. But as this concept builds on sexual racism, let me start there. Sociologist Charles Stember coined *sexual racism* in 1978 to capture how white people sexually reject people of color.[5] This rejection was a way to prevent interracial coupling, interracial cohabitation, and interracial sex. The point: Sexual practices and sexual desires are key components of maintaining racial hierarchies and white supremacy.[6] More specifically, two main forms of sexual racism are sexual rejection and sexual objectification.[7] For instance, people may reject Black or Asian men as potential partners based on stereotypes of Black men being hypersexual or Asian men being hypersubmissive, or people may only desire them through these fetishizing stereotypes.[8] Sexual racism shapes who is included or excluded as potential sexual or dating partners. It shapes who is considered attractive and desirable in society—with a premium placed on features and qualities associated with whiteness.[9] These sexual biases affect how people feel about themselves, how people engage in sexual and dating relationships, and how they engage more broadly with the world around them.

Sexual racism has consequences, though, outside of who gets fucked. Sexual racism maligns people of color and reinforces structural racism. For example, stereotypes of Black men being hypersexual "beast rapists"—symbolically violent in and of itself—have been used throughout U.S. history to justify slavery, lynching, race massacres, convict leasing, mass incarceration, and countless other structures of white supremacy.[10] Furthermore, stereotypes of Chinese women being hypersexual prostitutes led to the first restrictive federal immigration law in the United States—the Page Act of 1875—which effectively banned Chinese women from immigrating to the United States.[11] This act was not repealed until 1974. And even today, stereotypes of Mexican men being rapists (and drug dealers) fuel xenophobia and anti-immigration laws.[12] Sexual stereotypes about marginalized groups reinforce oppressive social structures.

I coin *sexual cissexism* to mean how prejudicial beliefs about trans people, including sexual stereotypes, can lead to sexual discrimination against trans people, including sexual rejection and sexual objectification. This sexual cissexism is rooted in the belief that cis people's gender is more natural and legitimate than trans people's gender, which leads to prejudice and discrimination against trans people.[13] A clear example of sexual cissexism and sexual rejection is that most people say that they would never date a trans person.[14] Sexual objectification, on the other hand, is how some people who do desire trans women and femmes often hypersexualize them as hyperfeminine and hypersubmissive pornographic sex objects.[15]

In this chapter, I argue that sexual cissexism works to maintain cisness. By placing a premium value on cisness, dominant understandings of sex, pleasure, desire, and sexual identities are constructed in and through cis understandings of gender and sexuality.[16] Sexual cissexism, then, represents a main mechanism of subordinating and marginalizing trans people, as it recenters heterosexual cisness as the desired norm within the larger society through constructing trans people as deviant or exceptional. But again, these sexual stereotypes have material consequences outside of who gets fucked. Antitrans legislators scapegoat trans people as pedophiles, for example, to deny trans people access to public spaces such as bathrooms partly based on these hypersexual stereotypes. Sexual cissexism also makes it difficult for trans people to find fulfilling and pleasurable relationships. Ultimately, if we want to achieve gender liberation and better pleasure and fulfillment for all people—but particularly for trans people—we must understand how and why sexual cissexism operates.

Heterosexual Cisness and Desiring Trans

Y'all, it was the pandemic. And who the hell knows how many online rabbit holes any of us went down during that time—but one of mine was Reddit. In April 2021, as I began conceptualizing the research for this book, I started downloading and reading Reddit threads about trans dating and trans sex. For three months, I collected over two hundred posts and their threads, some with thousands of comments. It was a lot to take in. In this section, I bring you down a Reddit rabbit hole with me to discuss how certain discourses about desiring trans people invest in and uphold sexual cissexism.

To note (and perhaps to warn you), while there were pleasurable and funny moments in the online land of Reddit, such as the satirical subreddit r/ChasersRiseUp, there were literally thousands of disturbing and discriminatory comments. Apparently, I often respond to this type of pain with sarcasm. And so, in this section, there will be a tone shift—both toward more internet lingo and in how I respond to and analyze these Reddit posts. I also italicize the Reddit posts for more ease of reading between my voice versus the Reddit voices. And while my tone might become more sarcastic (and hopefully pleasurable and funny!), these posts and the material presented are very serious—and they powerfully reflect how discourses around sex, sexuality, and desiring trans women and femmes maintain sexual cissexism and harm trans people.

So, without further ado, let's descend. One Reddit rabbit hole I went down was posts and threads by transamorous men.

Transamorous describes attraction toward trans people, especially trans women.[17] Transamorous partly emerged as a response to the *chaser*—someone who desires trans women through fetishizing, objectifying, and hypersexualizing them.[18] I guess, in a binary world, transamorous is supposed to refer to cis folks who desire but don't objectify or fetishize trans women. But the world is not a binary. And hence, one trans studies scholar noted how transamorous may just be the "gentleman's chaser,"[19] the "good guy" who claims an attraction toward trans women and femmes while still investing in and upholding sexual cissexism. Poster Under_score-, for example, begins: *"So, I'm straight. [. . .] But give me a minute to explain some things."* Lord, here we go. *"First, I'm down to have sex with women."* Well, thank you for letting us know that. *"I'm not attracted to men, and a TG has to be utterly feminine for me to be game."*

This post—in four short sentences—exemplifies how the sexual objectification component of sexual cissexism operates.[20] The poster begins by asserting his straight identity. He is clearly invested in his heterosexuality. But the poster also realizes that this straight identity needs explaining. Under dominant structures of sexual identity, which link sexuality to genitals, desiring a trans person can elicit questions about one's heterosexuality.[21] Under_score- works immediately to reassert his heterosexuality by telling us that he is "down to have sex with women." I presume he means cis women, as Under_score- refers to and marks trans women as "TG," discursively constructing trans women as different from cis women. Nonetheless, Under_score- ain't into men. Under_score- continues this work of reasserting his heterosexuality by claiming that trans women have "to be utterly feminine" for him "to be game." For many transamorous men, trans women are only desirable if they are hyperfeminine.[22] But this desire for hyperfemininity denies trans women the full range of womanhood and centers cis femininity as the norm to which trans women are compared. Trans women must be excessively feminine in relation to cis femininity. In just the beginning of his post, Under_score- shows how heterosexual cisness recenters itself at the expense of trans women and femmes.

Under_score- proceeds by playing devil's advocate with himself and says, *"But wait. You're not attracted to men? But TGs have a penis."* To which, Under_score- responds (to his own question), *"I'm attracted to the woman. The penis is really just something that is ignored."* I mean, some trans women may want their penis ignored, but uh, plenty don't. But okay, let's continue. *"At first it was kind of icky to me. But the sex is so exceptional that in time that extra penis in the mix is easily overlooked."* Any of us cringing and vomiting yet? *"As a bonus, a lot of the TGs that I've been with are some of the most attractive women that I've been with."*

Under_score- has now bought into two of the main stereotypes of trans women—hyperfeminine and hypersexual[23]—by discursively constructing trans women as exceptional and more attractive than cis women. Indeed, for Under_score-, because of that "icky extra penis" in the mix, it seems that trans women must be more sexually appealing and perform femininity better than cis women for Under_score- to feel secure in his cis heterosexuality. But this discursive maneuver in service to cis heterosexual masculinity yet again constructs trans women as different from cis women. Cis women remain the desired heterosexual norm in relation to which trans women must be exceptional. Under_score- uses *all* women as discursive objects to invest in and reassert his own cis heterosexual masculinity and his own pleasure.

Moreover, attraction, femininity, and womanhood are also bound up with racialized notions of desire. As scholars have shown, dominant ideas of beauty and attraction—and what it means to look "like a woman"—are often reflections of middle-class white femininity.[24] Feminine products are costly. Makeup isn't cheap. And skinny, blonde, and light skin color are often the dominant beauty images of the ideal woman.[25] Beauty norms, then, are a form of social and cultural capital less available to some groups, like poor women and women of color.[26] This discourse of being attracted to a particular type of femininity can exclude many women, especially lower-income trans women of color, who may not or cannot live up to dominant cis middle-class white expectations of womanhood.[27] This privileging of hyperfemininity and putting the burden on trans women to be "more attractive" than cis women represents a form of sexual cissexism that would push most trans women, especially poor trans women of color, outside of being seen as worthy of desire.

Just wait though. It gets better. He is about to give us a full-on point-by-point presentation about his attraction to trans women. *"Speaking of sex though,"* Under_score- continues, *"let me outline the reasons why I find TG sex so great."* Oh boy! I can only imagine how amazing this list is going to be. *"1. The sex is extremely intense. TGs have male hormones floating around in there. This means they have a male's sex drive and know exactly what a guy wants."* Ah, a biological essentialist framing. He then goes on to link this biological essentialism and hypersexualization to porn: *"They know how to pull off moves and poses that are usually only seen in pornography. Simply put, most TGs are wonderful nymphs."* Yes, gag. But now, we are about to get the juicy details. *"During intercourse, at first, you need to start slow. This makes me feel like I'm about to deflower a wonderfully tight virgin."* Note, it is about his feelings. *"The initial vulnerability is very sexy. Kissing makes it even more enhanced. The whole thing feels very naughty. Some of the TGs that I've been with know how to do kegels. The tactile sensation of this is heavenly."* But wait, there is still more. *"A lot of times I'm able to bring them to orgasm. No hands, only intercourse. This is a wonderful validation of my manhood. I've rarely brought women to orgasm this way. Sex with TGs is just easier."*

Under_score-'s post links the hypersexualization stereotype of trans women and femmes with hormones and biology. Men supposedly have a higher sex drive than women. And trans women supposedly still have these "male hormones." Of course, this discourse erases how hormones and sex drives vary among men and women.[28] Plenty of women have higher sex drives than many men. But this biological essentialist narrative also constructs trans women as inherently different from cis women through the idea that trans women supposedly still have some type of "male hormones" that shape their hypersexuality. This biological essentialism—the belief that biology and genes determine a person's most important characteristics—works to naturalize the hypersexual stereotype of trans women and femmes.

Moreover, assumptions about trans people's bodies, which are prevalent in these online spaces, ignore how transitioning can reshape bodies and ignore how trans people (whether transitioning or not) can experience their bodies and pleasure differently than cis people.[29] Many trans bodies are not like cis bodies. Some cis men, though, assume they have the same genitals and experience pleasure in similar ways as trans women. But transitioning can affect trans people's genitals and experiences of pleasure.[30] Gender dysphoria—when someone experiences distress because of an incongruence between their body and their gender—can also shape experiences of pleasure for some trans people during intimate encounters.[31] This assumption, then, about trans bodies upholds cis bodies as the norm in thinking about pleasure, erasing how trans people may experience pleasure differently. Nonetheless, this biological essentialist framing of trans people and of bodies has some cis men believing that they can understand and satisfy trans women better than they can satisfy cis women. Under_score- even gets erotically turned on by his masculinity being validated through easily satisfying some trans women. Women's orgasms often function as a masculine achievement for men, making them feel more masculine when they imagine that a woman orgasms during their sexual encounter.[32] In this instance, though, trans women become the hypersexual objects who serve as cis men's props to resolve their experience of not being able to sexually relate to or please cis women.[33] Everything is still all about his own pleasure and his cis heterosexual masculinity.

Indeed, number two on Under_score-'s list furthers this point of not liking cis women: "2. *It's cleaner. I know that sounds crazy, given where your penis is ending up. But most TGs have a cleaning method that does the trick.*" Oh, how kind of them. Sadly, though, he is about to get really misogynistic. So, I apologize in advance. "*Periods aside, most of the women that I've been with have some problem or another with their vagina. Either it's smell, feel, sensitivity, or appearance. I've been with a few women that had level ten vaginas. However, these don't compare to a clean tight hole that TGs can offer.*"

We might have to accept that a lot of straight dudes just don't like women.[34] And it seems some of them also hate vaginas. Indeed, the constant comparison of trans women to cis women has twin misogynistic effects. First, the strategy works to effectively devalue cis women. But it also works to recast trans women as different from cis women, whereby cis women are still the reference point for womanhood. In all scenarios, women are devalued; cis heterosexual masculinity and men's sexual pleasure are privileged and prioritized.

Let's keep it moving. "3. *The sexual dynamic: I love to dominate.*" Shocking. "*I like tiny chicks and chicks that play the innocent role. The emasculation that goes into TG sex is the ultimate form of submission.*" Surprise, surprise. "*They want to be a girl, be treated like a girl. It's hard to explain, but it's just hot beyond belief. In my opinion, TGs are extra girly just because of the effort that is involved in presenting themselves as a woman.*" And to put us out of our misery, point four: "*4. Can't get them pregnant.*"

Under_score- asserts a heterosexual superiority through positioning himself as the masculine man dominating the submissive trans woman. The poster essentializes trans women as inherently having had some type of masculinity that they have now given up. Under this logic, cis women do not have any type of masculinity to give up (as masculinity gets linked to biological essentialism); as such, cis women cannot fulfill Under_score-'s need to reach the ultimate heterosexual masculine superiority—which appears rooted in helping someone else supposedly relinquish masculinity. For some cis men who desire trans women, the hypersubmissive stereotype of trans women seems erotically charged with some notion of giving up masculinity (as if masculinity is something certain people—but not cis women—inherently and biologically possess). Through this process, trans women become props for heterosexual cisness and its own erotic needs and desires.

These desires and discourses are dangerous forms of sexual cissexism, as these discourses maintain cisness while still claiming to desire trans women. Notably, as notions of attractiveness, femininity, womanhood, and desirability are also bound up with notions of race and class, these processes of sexual cissexism can also maintain middle-class white femininity as the desired norm as well. In turn, these processes hurt and harm trans women and femmes, especially trans women and femmes of color. Rather than challenging dominant structures of gender, sexuality, and desire, these cissexist desires for trans women and femmes ultimately work to maintain the oppressive status quo and reveal how sexual objectification partly operates to uphold sexual cissexism. Trans women and femmes are denied being seen as people—are denied fulfilling sexual and romantic relationships. Instead, they are positioned as objects for validating cis heterosexual masculinity and cis men's pleasure. In positioning trans women and femmes as something exceptional or beyond the norms of desire, desire remains cis.

Sexual Cissexism and the Everyday Trans Dating and Sex Life

Like many young people in their twenties, Gabrielle used dating and hookup apps such as Grindr, Bumble, and Hinge to find and meet people for dates. For Gabrielle, though, the apps were often full of chasers. "You're bound to find a chaser there," Gabrielle matter-of-factly stated. "I usually don't get asked out on dates very often. I always get propositioned for sex or for someone to hook up with me. Outside of that, I usually don't get invited to restaurants or like to go out publicly." Gabrielle, who was single and in college, specifically mentioned how it seemed that cis men didn't want to be seen in public with trans women: "I think a lot of that could be with the men I've dated, like their own internalized homophobia, transphobia. But there's a lot of secrecy. They don't wanna be seen with you necessarily in public. Specifically in the South too." Too often, chasers and other cis men who desire trans women do not see trans women as potential romantic partners. Trans women are just sexual objects for cis men to use in the bedroom.[35] Secondary stigma could shape how and why some cis people may not pursue public relationships with trans people, as cis people don't want the stigma of dating or being with a trans person, whom our current society devalues.[36] Ideas about heterosexuality and sexual identity can shape this process as well, as Gabrielle's comment about "internalized homophobia, transphobia" suggests. Straight cis men may want to maintain others' assumptions of their heterosexuality by keeping their desires private—in the bedroom or in other private places where sex may occur—but not out in public on a date, where someone could question their sexuality or sexual identity. Heterosexual cisness remains the desired public norm by keeping desires for trans people in the private sphere.

When Gabrielle did go on dates with cis people, Gabrielle often spent the date educating them instead of having fun. In one instance, the guy had "a lot of questions," Gabrielle recalled. "He would ask me super-intrusive questions, like just the annoying, 'When did you have the surgery? Is your vagina made out of plastic? Or what does it look like?'" Gabrielle continued, "It's very much like they're really kind of focused immediately on my genitals. 'Do you have a vagina? Do you have a penis? How big is it? What does it look like?'" These discussions of genitals and surgery objectify and reduce trans people to their bodies instead of who they are as people. As Gabrielle detailed, "And that really kinda tells me it's rooted in a sexual nature that I'm being fetishized or something. But it always comes up. Like people wanna ask me a bunch of questions about it." In response, Gabrielle feels "like I have to play educator in the relationship or like 'welcome to my TED Talk,' and I'm giving them the whole presentation, like PowerPoint. It feels like I'm teaching instead of just on a date." This dynamic also extends to sex. "Sex with cis people, there's so many obstacles, and they don't know what to do or they're confused. 'What's the terminology? How should I refer to your body parts?' They're kind of like always in limbo, and I have to kind of reassure them or play educator," Gabrielle explained.

Trans folks may have to engage in emotional and other forms of labor when dating or hooking up with a cis person.[37] This labor can involve reassuring and educating cis people, and trans people may feel burdened explaining their bodies and gender to cis people, who don't have shared experiences.[38] And let's be real, educating someone about your body or identity while having sex or on a date is probably not the most erotic activity. Definitely doesn't seem hot. Doesn't seem pleasurable. A mood-killer, for sure.

To avoid this labor, many trans people in this study simply stopped dating and hooking up with cis people. And for trans people of color, they may avoid both cis and white people as potential dating and hookup partners. Indeed, research has shown that Black people in relationships with white people often have to educate their partners about racism.[39] Gabrielle—who is Black and Indigenous—preferred dating folks of color: "I don't like dating white people. It's just not for me dealing with like racism." Gabrielle often had a smoother and more enjoyable time with other trans folks as well, as trans people are often "caught up on my gender identity, my physical body." In not having to give a TED Talk or PowerPoint presentation, Gabrielle can discuss things that should matter on a date—hobbies, interests, goals, and life.

Importantly, these feelings about dating and hooking up with cis folks and white people emerge from real and sometimes horrifying experiences. For instance, Gabrielle discussed one evening of hooking up with a white cis dude. The man had roommates whom he didn't want to see Gabrielle, so they hooked up in the guy's car. "It was already like, okay, now I'm something you need to be ashamed of, you know? And it was mainly, I need to hide you," Gabrielle explained. The night didn't get any better, as painful hypersexualizing experiences unfolded in the car. "He was kind of having this assumption, maybe from a porn video he had watched or something, but it was just—he referred to me as a 'tranny,'" Gabrielle recollected. "Yeah, he called me a 'tranny,' 'transvestite,' and then referred to me as the term 'hooker.' And he is like, 'Yeah, you're gonna be my little hooker for tonight.' And I was like, you know, there was a lot of red flags." These hypersexualizing experiences intersected with racial fetishizing. "He referred to me as the term *hooker*. And so, it was interesting, he had referred to my penis as being a 'big black cock, BBC,'" Gabrielle disturbingly recalled. "Like racially profiling me, stereotyping me based off of stereotypes of what a Black person . . . But it's very much they perceive me as this Black man or a savage type of person who's super slutty, kinky, and is ready to have sex with anyone at any given second of the day." After ten minutes, Gabrielle ended the hookup. "I was like, 'Yeah, this isn't working.' [. . .] And I just like ended it there. But it was nasty."

Transmisogynoir is the intersection of transphobia, misogyny, and anti-Blackness.[40] And Gabrielle experienced hypersexualization and dehumanization through how sexual cissexism intersects with sexual racism. The racial fetishization and hypersexualization of Gabrielle's body and genitals made Gabrielle feel seen as a "Black man," delegitimizing Gabrielle's womanhood. These experiences greatly affected Gabrielle: "I felt kind of humiliated. I felt I wasn't really seen and heard and perceived to be human. The best way to describe it, I just felt like an inanimate object." Sexual cissexism and sexual racism shape Gabrielle's dating and sex life. Notably, as cisness relies on white middle-class understandings of gender (such as the ideal woman being skinny, blonde, and of light skin color),[41] sexual cissexism maintains and intersects with racism and other structures of oppression. These processes make navigating dating and hooking up difficult and painful for trans women and femmes, especially for trans women and femmes of color. These processes also dehumanize, objectify, and humiliate, while maintaining heterosexual cisness as the norm within society. Dominant desires remain cis; and trans folks experience a great deal of hurt and pain in navigating these dating and hookup landscapes. Gabrielle and other trans folks are not seen or heard for who they are as people. They are denied their full humanity—denied their full experiences of fulfillment and pleasure. Sexual cissexism materially harms trans lives.

Transphobia Without Transphobes

Sexual cissexism works in insidious ways to infiltrate our desires. And while some folks work to reassert their cis heterosexuality while desiring trans people, others seem terrified about how heterosexuality might be expanding to include trans people. To note, Under_score- and many men who desire trans women are straight. That is, straight men attracted to trans women are heterosexual, as trans women are women. But some people do not agree that heterosexuality should include attraction to trans people. And these folks have entered the scene to invent a new sexuality. A super heterosexuality! And this special heterosexuality—or at least the discourses around it—can reveal some logics of how the sexual rejection component of sexual cissexism operates.

"I made a new sexuality. It's called super straight," stated TikTok user KyleRoyce in February 2021. "Straight men like myself get called transphobic because I wouldn't date a trans woman. But that's not a real woman to me, I want a real woman. So now I'm super straight." A 20-year-old, white and Asian, heterosexual Zoomer, KyleRoyce is credited for coining the term "super straight." As he explained in his now viral TikTok video, "I only date the opposite gender—women that are born women. So you can't say I'm transphobic now because that's just my sexuality."

Super straight has become an identity adopted by some straight people who claim that they are not attracted to trans people. Indeed, since February 2021, the concept has diffused all over social media, from Twitter to Reddit to 4chan.[42] Right-wing groups also latched onto the idea, adopting the initials SS—signaling both super straight and Hitler's paramilitary *Schutzstaffel* from Nazi Germany. But in asserting SS as a sexual identity, super straights argue that their sexual desires are not transphobic. It is their sexuality. They were born that way. It is just who they are.

And while this super straight identity emerged in 2021, notably, heterosexuality, as an identity, emerged in the nineteenth century. As feminist scholar Jane Ward writes, "the terms *heterosexual* and *homosexual* did not exist until European physicians—all white men—coined and published them in medical journals in the late 1860s."[43] Heterosexual and homosexual behavior had, of course, existed before this time period. But now physicians, psychiatrists, and sexologists were classifying our sexual behaviors and attractions as a basis of our identity—as a basis of who we are.

But even before sexual behavior or attraction was ever considered the basis for identity, European imperialists and settlers justified violence, genocide, and colonization of communities and lands because Indigenous cultures held expansive notions of gender and sexuality that went against the Eurocentric gender binary and the man-woman-reproduction nuclear family norm.[44] Then, in the nineteenth and twentieth centuries, European physicians, including sexologists, invented heterosexuality as an identity and cultural ideal alongside white supremacist sciences such as craniometry and eugenics.[45] It is no coincidence that heterosexuality and homosexuality emerged at the same time as the end of slavery and the beginning of Jim Crow. As biological models of race such as phrenology were being undermined by growing evidence against this pseudoscience, new models of classifying people into groups constructed both interracial and homosexual desires as "abnormal" sexual object choices and threats to white superiority and the white nuclear family. Homosexuality—like interracial relationships—represented a cause of the perceived decline in white reproduction.[46] Heterosexuality became the norm not only to discipline people into reproducing but also to keep white people in intraracial relationships to reproduce for the white race.[47] Notably, then, the original invention of heterosexuality is also part of the history of race and white supremacy.[48] And we must situate the invention of super straights within this history of the invention of heterosexuality itself.

The Biological Essentialist Logics of SS

With the understanding that super straights emerged from this complicated historical context, let's meet some of these folks.[49] A

Reddit post by ggtab asks, "*Why is it okay for transgender people to call other people transphobic if they don't want to have sex with a transgender person? (not as rude as the ? sounds, read the full post).*" I guess we can continue reading, since ggtab has asked so nicely. The poster continues, "*Given the whole sex does not equal gender thing, this particular scenario confuses me to no end. I completely understand that in some cases, the reason may be down to transphobia, however I don't see that this is always the case. Let me use a heterosexual cisgender woman and a heterosexual transgender man as an example.*" We love an example!

The poster, in their example, gives some definitions: "*Heterosexuality: 'sexual attraction to people of the opposite sex.'*" Notice the word *sex*, which will become crucial to ggtab's argument about sexuality. "*Transgender: 'assigned gender does not correspond with birth sex.'*" Okay, an interesting definition of trans. "*Sex: 'either of the two main categories into which humans and most other living things are divided on the basis of their reproductive functions.'*" Ah, reproductive functions, another important point to note. "*I.e. sexuality is linked with biological sex, rather than gender identification.*" For ggtab and many super straights, sexuality is about biological sex.

Indeed, another poster, barbodelli, similarly states: "*The Super Straight movement is no surprise at all to me. If being straight is not enough to only be interested in members of the opposite biological sex. Then I guess call me super straight.*" And user DorianMaximus also writes, "*Idk why you are trying to deny science since gender and sex are two different things. You cannot change your chromosomes or your biological sex since they are permanent. [. . .] The issue is who people are attracted to, so it makes sense to focus on sex in this instance.*"

For these Reddit posters, gender is malleable, but sex is binary, immutable, and unchangeable. Sexuality, then, should be about attraction to biological sex, not gender or gender identification. This biological essentialist logic allows posters such as ggtab and DorianMaximus to claim a type of progressiveness for seeing trans people as the gender they are. Simultaneously, though, these posters also construct trans people as different—as outside of heterosexual desires—by claiming that sexuality is about sex, and sex is binary, biological, not a social construct, and different from gender. Like sociologist Eduardo Bonilla-Silva's *Racism Without Racists*—which explores how racial inequality persists despite people claiming to not be racists—biological essentialism becomes a frame, strategy, and logic that allows for transphobia without transphobes.[50] This frame naturalizes the sex binary, even though sex is not a binary, and this framing works to justify sexual rejection of trans people while simultaneously somewhat accepting them for the gender they are.

Indeed, for super straights, sexuality is only about this sex-based attraction. All other types of attraction—race, body size, height, or body parts, for instance—do not define sexuality. The problem with this approach to understanding human desire and identity, though, is that sex is an incoherent category. Sex comprises many things, including hormones, genitals, gonads, gametes, chromosomes, bone structure, reproductive capacity, physical appearance, and the list goes on. These elements of what we call "sex" do not neatly align, as plenty of people experience a wide variation of these characteristics.[51] Intersex people—people born with variations in their sex characteristics that do not fit the constructed sex binary of male and female—exist. For instance, there are people with XXY or XYY chromosomes, and there are people who have both ovarian and testicular tissues. Even gametes— which seem to be a main focus on defining biological sex lately[52]—

do not always universally couple with or determine other sex characteristics such as hormones and anatomy.[53] Some species also have both gamete types required for reproduction.[54] Sex is not binary. And people can experience wide variation in hormones, anatomy, body shape and appearance, and reproductive capacity.[55] Sex and sexuality do not and will not ever fit neatly into the male/female and hetero/homo binaries that we have created and that currently structure our society. Trying to discipline these categories denies the actual reality of their messiness.[56] It denies variation, which is a crucial component of biology.

Furthermore, along with dominant notions of sexual identity, the concept of biological sex is also rooted in the history of white supremacy and imperialism, whereby white people constructed themselves as more civilized than people of color and people in the Global South by arguing that white people were more sexually dimorphic and that sexual dimorphism was a sign of modernity.[57] That is, the notion of biological sex was born out of evolutionary science, whereby white scientists constructed white people as the most evolved for being the most sexually dimorphic.[58] This biological essentialist discourse erases all understanding of the colonial and racist roots of the invention of sex. Even today, these arguments have been used to deny African women such as Caster Semenya the opportunity to compete in Olympic sports for having traits associated with maleness.[59] So while some super straights may not engage in overt racism, their discursive strategies are rooted in white supremacist logics and concepts that try to justify not desiring trans people while not being seen as transphobic.

Nonetheless, ggtab, like many super straights, defines sex based on "reproductive functions," a logic that clings to the historical notion that heterosexuality should be about procreation.[60]

Sexual Cissexism [39]

Other Reddit posters, though, push back against this idea. In one instance, Reddit poster mazotori, who is "a trans person who is usually T4T," states, *"That's . . . not how attraction works? Like are you gonna try and tell me as straight men can sense infertility issues?? Or are not attracted to women over 35??"* As implied by mazotori, the logic of reproduction in regard to heterosexual desire ignores that there are cis men and cis women who cannot reproduce either; and yet, most people would still see them as men and women (or, to use sex terms, still see them as male and female). Nonetheless, in privileging reproductive functions, ggtab constructs sexuality as attraction to sex and genitals: *"If we were to say that the heterosexuality of a person must include transgender people, regardless of the genitals and reproductive functions they possess, then surely that wipes out the whole concept of sexuality too?"*

In sexualized, intimate settings, biology-based criteria, especially with a heightened focus on genitals, are often used to assess and discriminate against trans people, especially trans women.[61] That is, biological essentialist discourses frame some of these justifications for discrimination. But on some level, I agree with ggtab. Transness does trouble dominant understandings of heterosexuality and sexual identities. For instance, if heterosexuality is linked to genitals, transness disrupts that link. A problem with sexual identity is that the concept often privileges genitals as one's sexual object choice and promotes this sexuality as biological, self-evident, and natural.[62] Transness destabilizes sex, gender, sexuality, and desire as it can reveal how these categories are not inherent, biological, and self-evident. As mazotori even pushes back, folks aren't really attracted to biology—how can someone see infertility or chromosomes or even genitals when they experience attraction toward someone? Transness can make us call into question what exactly we are attracted to and how that attraction is much more complicated than identity, genitals, reproduction, gender, and sex. Super straights, though, try to reinvest in biology—while ignoring the complexities and history of biology—in order to make the sex binary and sexual identities appear inherent and natural (which they are not).

"Born This Way" Discourses

This notion of biological sex and its link to sexuality is pervasive, even emerging in the mainstream gay rights movement rhetoric that people are "born this way"—that same-sex attraction is natural, inherent, and unchangeable. Super straights often use this same discourse to reify and rationalize their superior heterosexuality. As Reddit poster babno states, *"How can an orientation be transphobic? People are born that way, they can't help it."* Other Reddit posters take up this logic to argue that their sexuality—characterized specifically by not being attracted to trans people—is biological, and hence, neither discriminatory nor something to be ashamed of. *"No, because I shouldnt be shamed for my sexuality,"* writes poster DeltaMx11. *"I have as much of a right to be not attracted to a transgender person as a gay man has a right not to be attracted to a woman or a lesbian has the right not to be attracted to a man. I have no personal problem with transgender people, but I cant force myself to be attracted to a biological man with a female brain."* Similarly, user doorknoob posts, *"I'm not sexually attracted to transgender people. There shouldn't be stigma for being heterosexual."* And in giving us a super straight rallying cry, user Dontwanttogooglethat even exclaims, *"Fight the good fight! Down with superphobes!"*

In adopting antishame, antistigma, and "born this way" discourses, straight posters on Reddit use mainstream gay rights rhetoric to argue that they are naturally, biologically, inherently uninterested in dating or having sex with trans people. But in a society that privileges heterosexuality, there is no actual shame for being straight; straight people do not face isolation and stigma for their heterosexuality. That is, this discursive move around shame and stigma misses how stigma is about possessing a marginalized position or identity within the broader contexts of society, erasing the power dynamics of sex and sexuality that underlie compulsory heterosexuality.[63] This concept of "superphobes" also misses power dynamics—cis people do not experience structural discrimination and violence for their cisness.

These social media posts, though, point to the limits of "born this way" discourses and biological essentialist notions of sexual identity. In the 2000s, when the mainstream gay rights movement was focused on marriage equality and parents sending their queer kids to conversion camps, biological arguments around being gay were an appeal to the empathy of straight people—no one would choose a life of discrimination (i.e., choose being gay); therefore, homosexuality must be biological.[64] This strategy hinges on an investment in biological authority to claim legitimacy and on the legal argument that being discriminated against for having an innate characteristic should make gay people a protected class. Notably, however, turning to biology does not actually guarantee legitimacy. Biological arguments—namely, eugenics—have been used to demean and subordinate marginalized groups by categorizing them as innately inferior, and thereby justifying medical experimentation, sterilization, systemic discrimination, and genocide.[65] In other words, biological claims can easily serve to bolster eugenicist arguments. Plenty of white cisgender men have often thought they were biologically superior to other groups of people and used biological arguments to justify their status and privilege.[66] If gayness, then, is biological, it can become pathologized, a disease or disorder to cure, not to be accepted or celebrated.[67]

Moreover, to be born gay or straight assumes not only that someone is biologically attracted to men or women but that gender categories themselves—men and women—are also natural, obvious, inherent, unchanging, and biological.[68] To say you are biologically attracted to men would assume that there is also something biological about the category of *man* to which you are attracted. In relying then on gender essentialism, "born this way" rhetoric harms trans people,[69] becoming another discursive strategy for expressing transphobia. Intriguingly and insidiously, super straights adopted a strategy used to expose inequality—gay rights activists saying they were "born this way"—to reassert heterosexuality as superior and to entrench biases against trans people, while claiming to not be transphobic.

Personal Preference as the New Transphobia

Then, there is assolf_shitler, an exemplar of the super straights using notions of personal preference to justify not desiring trans people. This user begins: *"Or at least it's not more prejudiced than for any other trait. It's just the same as someone not liking brown hair even though they find the other person attractive otherwise, and would date them if that person dyed their hair blond."* Continuing this personal preference logic, assolf_shitler states, *"Besides, when dating, prejudice doesn't matter. That's one area where no one has the right to complain about it. Whether it's racial prejudice, trans prejudice (not the same as transphobia) etc. you can be disappointed but if you're upset about it you're being entitled."*

In addition to biological essentialism and "born this way" rhetoric, "personal preference" discourse has often been used to rationalize or defend sexual and romantic rejection of certain groups of people. Reddit poster assolf_shitler explicitly makes the comparison to having a racial preference—which similarly "doesn't matter," as assolf_shitler asserts. But having a racial preference does matter, and this personal preference discourse often erases the racist cultural assumptions that shape desire and attraction.[70] Indeed, personal preference discourses around race have contributed to social and cultural white supremacy, as sexually stereotyping people of color or excluding them from desirability maintains whiteness as the most desirable race.[71] Personal preference around race, then, is another discursive strategy to use more language that is not explicitly racist, but that maintains racial inequality and hierarchies.[72] In these contexts, "personal preference" becomes another framing of transphobia without transphobes.

Moreover, when assolf_shitler—notably yet another reference to Nazism—compares trans prejudice to hair color prejudice, this poster erases the larger structural, social, and cultural factors shaping desire and ignores how these dating prejudices can extend into other areas, like the discrimination trans people face in the workplace or in the public sphere. In replying to assolf_shitler, LibraryLass states, *"Except that, generally, no one is murdering their partner for not being a natural blonde. No one is trying to legislate what bathrooms brunettes can use. No one considers brunettes to categorically be sexual deviants."* LibraryLass deconstructs the personal preference discourse to show how these desires relate to larger structural and political battles.

Nonetheless, super straights use logics—biological essentialism, "born this way," and personal preferences—that maintain sexual cissexism through a deep investment in heterosexuality and sexual identities. Cunningly, these logics privilege cis desires and malign trans desirability while claiming to eschew transphobia. They also work to normalize the wholesale sexual and romantic rejection of trans people. These logics reveal, though, the intimate connection between heterosexuality (and sexual identities more broadly) and maintaining sex and gender binaries. Sexual cissexism allows people to invest in heterosexuality and sexual identities while ignoring the ultimate consequences of that investment—harming trans people and denying them their full humanity.

Challenging Sexual Cissexism

Many trans women and femmes have to navigate sexual cissexism in their dating and sex lives. This sexual cissexism can take the form of sexual objectification that reinvests in heterosexual cisness, while casting trans women and femmes as exceptional but outside the norms of dominant cis desires. This sexual cissexism can also take the form of sexual rejection that invests in biological essentialism and cisness in order to exclude trans people from desirability altogether. These processes also intersect with sexual racism to maintain cis middle-class notions of whiteness as the desired norms as well. Either way, whether through objectification or rejection, trans people are denied their full humanity—denied their full experiences of fulfillment and pleasure. And as pleasure is a measure of freedom—that is, people deserve relationships and satisfactions that are life-enriching[73]—sexual cissexism is a roadblock to gender liberation.

But trans folks also find strategies to challenge sexual cissexism or at least avoid it in their dating and sex lives. "The few trans folks

I've been with, it's been very positive experiences where I felt respected, seen," Gabrielle stated. "I didn't feel like I was being looked at like a sex toy or something. I was a person. Yeah, it was more easy. I felt safe. It was smooth. I didn't have to try so hard. They didn't have to. We felt very comfortable, and we felt very safe with one another." Gabrielle went on to give a more specific example. "I'm thinking back to like the really affirming hookups I've had with other trans people. And like being seen by them. And they were seeing like beautiful traits about me that I don't like about myself," Gabrielle recalled. "Like I have really broad shoulders. And so, the trans man I was with was like complimenting me on aspects of my body that I usually don't feel comfortable with. And it felt really nice."

The next two chapters—on comfort and t4t—turn to how relationships and other dating and hookup strategies can challenge sexual cissexism. These chapters examine how trans folks resist and make space for themselves, how they find safety and respect, and how they feel seen. As these chapters will show, comfort and relationships with other trans people help us chart paths toward gender liberation and sexual freedom. They help us chart paths to finding pleasure that may challenge dominant social structures. And they help us chart paths to challenging sexual cissexism and the harm that cisness wreaks on trans lives.

3 *Comfort and the Paradox of Pleasure*

Comfort. A state of physical ease and freedom from pain or constraint.[1]

Comfortable. Providing physical ease and relaxation.[2]

Some examples from this study:[3] *Comfortable communicating. Comfortable with sharing. A sensation of comfort just being around them. Comfortable in my skin. Comfortable in your own body. Comfortable with one's self. Comfortable being trans. Comfortable in who you are. Comfortable with one another. Feels most comfortable. Feels really comfortable. Comfortable and on the same page. A level of comfortability. Comfortable and safe. Comfortable around. Comfortable with that. Vulnerability requires that kind of comfort. What's your comfort level? If you don't feel comfortable answering any questions, feel free to skip. Comfortable talking about what you're interested in sexually. Comfortable bottoming. Comfortable both bottoming and topping. Comfortable to explore outside of your comfort zone. Comfortable with physical contact. Comfortable just walking around. Comfortable out in public. Comfortable setting boundaries. Comfortable giving you my address. Do I feel more comfortable going to their place? Comfortable to meet up in person. Are you comfortable with this? This is what I'm com-*

fortable with. I don't feel comfortable doing that. Comfortable with you. I just feel more comfortable.

Comfort. A word often mentioned in passing, but rarely a focus of sociological research. A concept often not centered in how we theorize about sex, sexuality, and gender. An idea not taken very seriously by scholars in examining social life.

Comfort. The pleasant and satisfying feeling of being physically or mentally free from pain and suffering. Or something that provides this feeling.[4]

Comfort. A mode of relation—a measure of freedom.

The Comfort Turn

There have been some important and critical scholarly turns in recent years. In sexualities studies, there has been the "pleasure turn," which has centered pleasure in understanding sex, sexuality, and social life.[5] This turn has been a corrective to the typical focus on health, disease, and sex negativity within sexualities research.[6] This turn is also part of a larger agenda of understanding pleasure as a measure of freedom.[7] All people need and deserve pleasure—that satisfaction and enjoyment that is life-enriching. A goal, then, in striving for liberation is changing our social structures to maximize people's experiences of pleasure.[8]

In trans studies, there has also been a joy and euphoria turn. The concept of "euphoria" comes from the trans community to describe positive emotions, including joyful feelings about one's gender.[9] Euphoria and joy are correctives to medical and social scientific approaches that focus on dysphoria and pathologizing trans people. This corrective also pushes back on trans people being reduced to just experiences of distress and discrimination.[10]

Instead, joy and euphoria highlight positive possibilities of trans lives, relationships, and communities. Joy and euphoria help to capture the fuller complexities of the everyday trans life. And while these scholarly shifts in sexualities studies and trans studies have been important in providing more nuanced depictions of people's lives, we need to critically interrogate these concepts themselves. Pleasure, joy, and euphoria are complicated feelings and processes that are also bound up with power: An oppressor might get pleasure from oppressing, a bully might get joy from bullying, and a docile subject—such as an employee who gets pleasure in working long hours for their boss—might get joy from internalizing dominant norms. Pleasure can be paradoxical. It can challenge dominant structures. For instance, trans pleasure can disrupt cisness. But pleasure can also uphold dominant structures as well (such as when cis men get pleasure in fetishizing trans women in order to reaffirm their own cis heterosexual masculinity). Pleasure is complicated.

This chapter turns to the messiness of sex, sexuality, language, and bodies in trans women's and femmes' lives in order to examine the complexities of pleasure and joy. In doing so, this chapter proffers perhaps another turn—the comfort turn. Indeed, the word *comfort* came up constantly with the trans women and femmes interviewed for this study. Nearly every trans person mentioned the word at some point during the interview, showcasing how comfort is central to how people experience and navigate dating, sex, hooking up, desire, pleasure, joy, and euphoria. One might even say comfort is foundational to the types of pleasure and joy that do not hurt, harm, and oppress. Comfort, moreover, is a mode of relation that is crucial for care, communication, consent, and community. And comfort is pivotal for achieving gender liberation and sexual freedom. But despite how important comfort is in experiencing and giving pleasure and despite how crucial comfort can be to social relations, including within sexual relations, we know little about this concept. This chapter, then, examines comfort to see how it may be an antidote to cisness and compulsory heterosexuality. This chapter also explores how comfort may be where many great pleasures reside.

Discomfort, Disregard, and Disrespect

"Being on hormones, my dick doesn't work that often," stated 24-year-old Carmen. "It's weird to call it a dick, but I feel like a lot of times I don't talk about her in these conversations." A Puerto Rican Pisces, Carmen navigated dating and hooking up with the ease of any good water sign. This casual approach was often necessary for trans women and femmes who hooked up with cis people. As Carmen explained, "I think there's guys who explicitly want a trans girl who has a functioning penis, and like, I'm on hormones. I've had Viagra prescribed to me by my medical provider, but I don't use it all the time. And let alone, even if I use it, not a lot comes out. I don't cum a lot."

Cis people often don't know much about trans bodies. And trans bodies—particularly if a person is medically transitioning—are not like cis bodies. Part of transitioning for trans women and femmes can include skin softening, increased genital sensitivity, differences in sexual function, and even new sources of sexual pleasure away from their genitals and toward new erogenous zones such as nipples, legs, and backs.[11] As another interviewee Sabi said, "I mean, honestly, at this point—this might be TMI, so stop me—but at this point, estrogen has done to my ability to top what the oil rigs have done to the Texas rural community. They've decimated it." It can be hard to get hard.

For Carmen, these bodily changes make it feel strange to even call Carmen's genitalia a "dick." This comment could hint at different things. For instance, it could hint at gender dysphoria. Gender dysphoria is when people experience distress because of an incongruence between their body and their gender.[12] To note, gender dysphoria comes from cisness. If we didn't assign gendered meanings to bodies, then people would probably not experience an incongruence between their body and gender. (And, to make another note, cis people experience gender dysphoria too—such as cis men feeling an incongruence between their body and dominant ideas of masculinity and wanting to take steroids and build more muscle in order to be perceived as more masculine, or cis women feeling an incongruence between their body and ideas of femininity and wanting to be skinny in order to live up to dominant middle-class white beauty ideals.) The point is: In a cis society, such as ours, we have assigned gendered meanings to bodies. And these meanings can shape how we experience our bodies. Moreover, we have assigned gendered meanings to genitals, whereby penis is often associated with man and vagina is often associated with woman. We also have few options beyond the binary language of penis and vagina to describe genitals. In turn, folks whose bodies do not align with these dominant cis understandings of gender and genitals may experience distress. In response, trans people may assign a different gendered meaning to their genitals and to other body parts as a strategy to avoid dysphoria.[13] Carmen calling the dick "her" could be a way to manage this distress.

Carmen's comment, though, could also hint at how hormones make the penis something else—something we don't quite have the language for yet and something a lot of cis folks still don't understand. Indeed, trans people often redefine words used to describe body parts, including genitalia.[14] This strategy of assigning new meanings to gender and genitals can become a way to reclaim one's body outside of medical narratives.[15] That is, this reconfiguration through regendering genitals can challenge the notion that trans people's bodies are in conflict with their gender.[16] This regendering can also lead to congruence. Through these processes, then, new ways of understanding gender, genitals, and the body that challenge cisness and compulsory heterosexuality can emerge.

Carmen was comfortable enough to educate cis folks about these topics and about trans bodies. The problem was when people (well, cis men really) did not respect Carmen. In recalling a hookup, Carmen stated, "He was trying to touch my dick, basically. And it was like really weird 'cause I wasn't really down for that." This weirdness was partly related to the fact that Carmen had already told this guy via text what Carmen wanted and didn't want. In ignoring this information, he disrespected Carmen. "So, I've had experiences where they're asking for that persistently, and especially if we agree to not do that over text, but then when we meet in person, you're still being persistent about that, I think that in itself just feels weird," Carmen explained. "If you're disregarding the information that I'm giving you, I don't think that you're truly respecting who I am and what I'm going through."

Carmen communicated, and communication is key to creating comfort and building respect. Notably, some trans people may feel burdened explaining their bodies and gender to cis people.[17] But Carmen personally didn't seem to mind this labor. Carmen often educated potential hookups—via texts—about trans bodies and about Carmen's own sexual wants, needs, and desires. Communicating via dating apps or text can provide a level of comfort and safety in discussing sex, bodies, and desires.[18] This man, though, disregarded Carmen's educational labor and sexual needs. This disrespect—through ignoring Carmen's education and communication—breaks trust and precludes comfort. Rather, it creates discomfort. Moreover, this disrespect disregards Carmen's lived experiences in the service of centering and privileging cis wants, needs, and desires. These acts also further the dehumanization of trans women and femmes, especially trans women and femmes of color such as Carmen, who may also have to navigate being racially fetishized and sexually objectified.[19] This disrespect can also lead to physical assault, including unwanted sexual touch. Disrespect is the antithesis of building comfort.

R-E-S-P-E-C-T: Find Out What Comfort Means

Carmen further discussed respect in relation to comfort and dating. "When thinking about dating, the first thing that comes to mind is actually—and I think a lot of people trans or not—it's about seeking respect," Carmen explained. "Do you respect me as the transgender woman that is in front of you? Or is there a deeper agenda?" Carmen said that playing this "guessing game of if I'm gonna be respected or if I'm gonna be fetishized" keeps Carmen's "guard up" when navigating the dating and hookup landscape. "I do make it clear that I'm not into people, specifically men, who are discreet or on the down low," Carmen stated. "I think that has been a lesson learned throughout my transition is that not to waste my time there. 'Cause most times, I'm gonna be disrespected, and I'm gonna feel used."

Carmen, who was single during the time of the study, went on to describe a cis guy whom Carmen casually dates and who shows respect and provides comfort. On one date, Carmen and this man went to McGuane Park in Chicago. Afterwards, they had dinner in Chinatown, "and after that, we had shared a kiss." However, because of past experiences of men wanting to keep Carmen "a secret," Carmen worried about this public display of affection. Carmen asked this man if he was okay being affectionate in public: "And I'm just like, 'Okay, well, you're not nervous holding my hand out in public like this?' And he would always assure me that it's not anyone else's business what we're doing."

These moments of respect made Carmen experience euphoric comfort. "I feel the most pleasure when I don't have to worry," Carmen noted. "If a person makes me feel comfortable during the date, and I'm able to lower my guard down, I think that in itself is like . . . it's kind of euphoric in a way where I could feel comfortable in who I am." This pleasure and euphoria emerge from feeling comfort, safety, and respect, and being affectionate in public. As Carmen explained, "Being told that my life was safe and that I didn't have to fear being disrespected or feeling like I couldn't hold his hand or that we couldn't share a kiss out in public. Yeah, I think it's definitely that."

Respect is a way to validate trans people's identities and treat them according to their needs.[20] For Carmen, respect was the opposite of fetishization, which dehumanizes and objectifies trans people, especially trans women of color.[21] This binary, though, of seeking respect versus avoiding fetishization often shapes how Carmen and other trans women and femmes navigate dating and hooking up. Trans folks keep their guard up and stay alert in these situations to be safe and to avoid people who may fetishize and objectify them. Notably, trans women report being at a higher risk of violence compared to cis women, and trans women of color report being at a higher risk of violence, including sexual and intimate partner violence, compared to both white trans women and cis women.[22] In turn, trans women of color, such as Carmen, have to be particularly cautious while dating or hooking up. On the other hand, when Carmen felt safe and reassured by a partner, Carmen experienced pleasure and euphoria. Many trans people often link euphoria to positive emotions of having one's identity affirmed.[23] Carmen, though, connected this euphoria and pleasure to comfort, to not having to worry, to being respected, to being accepted. Respect—validating someone and their needs—is an important part of building comfort. And comfort—the freedom from worry— is where pleasure begins to burgeon.

Comfort and Sexual Positioning

Comfort can also shape sexual experiences, including challenging cis heterosexual ideas about sexual positioning. "There's times where I don't want to have anal sex, and I don't wanna get fucked," Carmen explained. "I consider myself versatile. But I feel like as a trans woman, most guys are seeking for someone who bottoms." Because of cis stereotypes about gender and sex, many folks (or at least many cis men) assume women, including trans women, should be penetrated, even if that is not what they want or what brings them pleasure. This cis assumption is shaped by larger ideas that to be a woman is to be penetrated. "I've had guys who have said that they're gonna make me into the woman that I want to be,"

Carmen recounted, "and I'm just like, I make myself into the woman that I am. I don't need you to fuck me so that you could help me become any more of a woman than I already am."

Sex acts are just sex acts; they only have meaning because people have assigned meaning to them. In a cis society, binary ideas about sex and gender often shape the meaning of sex acts themselves, including sexual positioning. Carmen mentioned how cis men often seek a trans woman who bottoms. Bottoming—taking the anal receptive position—is often seen as the feminine position in comparison to topping, an act often configured as the masculine position. This perception upholds patriarchal heterosexual understandings of gender and sexuality as it associates being penetrated with submissiveness, womanhood, and femininity.[24] Race can shape these gendered meanings of sexual positioning as well. Within gay communities, for example, some gay men often assume Black men are tops and Asian men are bottoms.[25] These racialized sexual positioning stereotypes can limit pleasure, especially if someone feels compelled to take a sexual position that they don't necessarily want to take.

Another interviewee for this study, 23-year-old Emily from Riverside, California, further explained, "I just like to bottom. I like bondage a lot, for instance, and I like to bottom in those instances. I like to top, too, so I'm versatile. But I think being transgender, I'm able to do that and be comfortable in my body because I can bottom and feel comfortable." Emily, who was a part-time photographer during the time of the study, went on to compare bottoming now to in the past: "Because when I was a cis guy, I wouldn't feel comfortable bottoming. Whereas like as a trans woman, I'm comfortable both bottoming and topping. At first, I wasn't ready with topping just because I think of internalized transphobia, but I think now I am. And, yeah, it's a lot of fun." As topping is often associated with masculinity, Emily didn't feel comfortable bottoming until Emily transitioned. Notably, Emily is white, and thus didn't have to simultaneously navigate the racial stereotypes of sexual positioning. But gendered ideas of sex acts can still influence people and prevent them from sexual exploration and pleasure. After transitioning, Emily first only bottomed, which Emily partly associated with internalized transphobia. This comment alludes to the profound dominance of cis heterosexual ideas about sex and sexuality, which make some trans women and femmes think that the only proper way to be a woman is to be penetrated. Eventually, though, Emily, who was currently single, found comfort and freedom in being trans and in sexually exploring both topping and bottoming. Emily also mentioned bondage, which can allow for exploring gender, pleasure, and erotic sensations through experimentation.[26] Bondage and comfort can allow people to explore and even challenge cis heterosexual ways of thinking about sex, bodies, gender, and pleasure.

To note, dominant cis ideas about gender can shape pleasure, even for trans women. The previous chapter on sexual cissexism showed how cis men get pleasure from fucking trans women and how this pleasure is partly bound up in reaffirming their cis heterosexual masculinity.[27] Some trans women get pleasure from bottoming as well, such as 26-year-old Winnie, another white trans woman in this study. Living in Madison, Wisconsin, while currently in a nonmonogamous relationship, Winnie shared, "In negotiations, talking about what specific activities we're gonna do, I'd say me being trans definitely does have a role in that, like the reason I'm mainly a bottom is because I get some level of gender euphoria from it just because, even though it's dumb that this is the case, bottoming is seen as more feminine." For Winnie and some other trans people in this study, they may get pleasure and euphoria from these gender stereotypes of sex acts and sexual positioning—even as they realize that this euphoria comes from these larger gender stereotypes prescribed by cis society. Pleasure, including sexual pleasure, is complicated.

It is important, however, to expand pleasure beyond gender and racial stereotypes and cis heterosexual ways of thinking so that people can experience the full pleasurable possibilities of their bodies. It is also important to expand ideas of pleasure so that people don't feel pressured or obligated to uphold these stereotypes during sex. As Carmen stated, womanhood is not defined as getting fucked by a man. This resistance pushes back at dominant cis heterosexual ways of thinking about sex, gender, and sexuality; moreover, it can expand sexual pleasure beyond just thinking about sex as men penetrating women.

Comfort and Sexual Pleasure

Comfort can allow for this fuller exploration of pleasure. Returning to the cis man with whom Carmen had a wonderful, euphoric, and comfortable date, Carmen also had amazing sex with him, including just the day before being interviewed for this study. "There's just this way that I love being grabbed," Carmen stated, "and I think being on 'mones has helped my body become more sensitive to things. And especially when I look at myself in the mirror, I love how my body looks." Carmen continued, "So, when it comes to hooking up, I feel like when I had sex with him last night . . . like we were having sex in a way where it felt like cuddling. I felt like I was being held." This pleasure was rooted in comfort and care, not necessarily in genitals, penetration, or the dominant ways society often frames sexual pleasure. "And I think that one thing that I really enjoy from him is that he knows how I like my breasts to be touched, and he'll like caress my body, he'll caress my breasts," Carmen explained. "'Cause it's like, again, I won't always have an orgasm, but I feel like when I do, it plays a lot into like how I'm feeling pleasured or how I'm feeling a lot of release passionately."

Hormones shaped Carmen's sexual comfort and bodily confidence. Studies have shown that hormone therapy can lead to greater sexual satisfaction for trans people, partly through improved body satisfaction.[28] One's sex drive can also increase, which can improve comfort and confidence in one's body.[29] Furthermore, Carmen's comfort with this man and the way he explores Carmen's body also brings pleasure. This pleasure wasn't necessarily about penetration but about exploring the body in affirming and caring ways.

Sabi, a 22-year-old, Southeast Asian, full-time college student living in Santa Barbara, California, also discussed how comfort and discomfort shape sexual interactions with and for trans people. "A lot of trans people have a lot of big stuff about where they like to be touched, and what they like in particular. For me, I'm lucky enough that I don't have any particular genital dysphoria," stated Sabi, who was in a committed relationship during the time of the study. "I know a lot of people do, so whenever I'm hooking up with someone, I do ask, 'Hey, is there any part of you that you don't want me to interact with?' Yeah, I think that would actually be the big thing is setting the ground rules of what they're comfortable with in terms of dysphoria," Sabi explained. "Because that can be the second emergency stop on a train—if you touch parts that they feel very uncomfortable about, you can just cause the entire thing to slam shut, and it doesn't work out great for either person." Historically, the dominant medical model of transsexuality was about repressing or denying a sexuality. A "true" trans person was supposed to have a disgust toward their own genitals—they were supposed to have gender and genital dysphoria.[30] Gender dysphoria, though, is a medicalized term that comes from psychiatry. Today, under the *Diagnostic and Statistical Manual of Mental Disorders (DSM)*, trans people still often have to get diagnosed with gender dysphoria in order to access gender-affirming medical care.[31] But the *DSM* framing of dysphoria is part of upholding a dominant narrative that trans people must experience distress about their gender, genitals, and body.[32] This term can also pathologize gender diversity, as it often only focuses on negative feelings such as distress in understanding trans experiences.[33]

Sabi challenges the notion that all trans people experience genital dysphoria, as Sabi does not. Sabi, however, is also aware that trans people are not a monolith—they have different needs and experiences around sex and their bodies. For trans people who experience dysphoria around their genitals, it can be common to avoid certain types of intimacy as a strategy to avoid distress.[34] Communication and comfort, then, can help to shift sexual aspects away from things that are uncomfortable (such as touching genitals) and to things more comfortable (such as being close).[35] Sabi uses sexual communication to make sure that Sabi's sexual partners are comfortable. This sexual communication can foster more satisfying relationships and better sexual experiences.[36] Communication, then, is part of feeling comfortable, and comfort is often crucial to fulfilling sexual experiences. As Sabi noted, if discomfort arises, it can be a mood killer for all involved.

Quinn, a 21-year-old, full-time college student from Goleta, California, also discussed sexual communication, comfort, and the freedom of decentering genitals in experiencing pleasure. As Quinn, who is white and who had two partners at the time of the interview, explained, "Typically before engaging in sex with someone, I discuss where I have dysphoria around. Like, I have dysphoria specifically around my genitals, and I dislike using and having sustained contact with my genitals in sexual situations." The first time Quinn had sex after coming out as lesbian, Quinn recalled, "That was a very liberating experience, because there was no pressure to interact in that way, that I was not being asked to use my genitals, I was using them of my own will and to the extent I was comfortable using them."

Dominant understandings of sex and sexuality (and even race) are often genital-centered. Sex is often thought of as penis and vagina. And race-based sexual stereotypes can also reduce people of color to their genitals with the racist assumption that Hispanic people and Black people have large penises and are hypersexual.[37] For some trans people, though, decentering genitals during sex can open up pleasure to other bodily experiences.[38] Comfort and communication can be essential to exploring these other pleasurable possibilities beyond genitals and stereotypes. That is, comfort can expand notions of sex and pleasure. Comfort can also be hot. It can be sexy. It can even be orgasmic. And comfort shows how communication and care are erotic, pleasurable, and enjoyable. Comfort can challenge cis heterosexual ways of thinking about sex and pleasure. And by moving sex away from stereotypes and an over-focus on genitals, comfort can challenge racist sexual stereotypes about people of color as well. In doing so, comfort can be liberating.

Comfort and Sexual Identities

In addition to sexual positioning and sexual pleasure, identities, including sexual identities, are also bound up with experiences of comfort. "I say that I mostly date cis men," Carmen explained. "They don't always have to be straight. I honestly prefer if I am dating a man that he is pansexual or even bisexual. I think it makes it just a little comforting sometimes." Carmen found comfort in partnering with nonheterosexual cis men. And among the trans women and femmes in this study who did date or hook up with cis dudes, many preferred queer cis guys. As 32-year-old Chic—another interviewee—explained, "I cannot imagine dating somebody that is not queer in some way. I cannot. They may not necessarily have to be trans, but they need to be in the LGBTQ+ somewhere." For Chic, LGBTQ people are often "very comfortable" around other queer and trans people, whereas with straight people, "there's always a little bit of barrier where it's like, 'Oh, I'm being too queer for you,' or something like 'I'm being too trans' or 'too gay' or whatever."

Queerness can create comfort, even between cis and trans folks. From Carmen's experience, many straight men were "down low" and wanted to keep Carmen a secret. "Down low" is often a racialized term used to pathologize straight-identified Black and Latino men's same-sex attraction and behavior, but plenty of white men may engage in nondisclosure about their sexuality as well.[39] And for some cis men—of any race—who think that their sexuality may get questioned for desiring trans women and femmes, they may want to keep these desires private to maintain a public appearance of heterosexuality. In relegating desires for trans people to the private sphere, heterosexuality and cisness remain the dominant norms within the larger society.[40] Trans women and femmes such as Carmen and Chic resist by preferring queer cis men. They find comfort in some level of queerness. In other words, sexual identities shape how Carmen, Chic, and other trans women and femmes experience comfort with cis men.

Heterosexuality, though, isn't the only identity that affects these relationship dynamics. A gay identity can create discomfort for some trans women and femmes as well. For instance, 19-year-old Lin—a Chinese college student living in Riverside, California—talked about how the language a partner uses during sex can be invalidating. "When my boyfriend and I started having sex for the first couple of times, he just wasn't quite aware of the terms he should use," Lin explained. "Sometimes the terms he came up with was, 'Oh, we're having like gay sex,'" to which Lin replied, "'That's not the case. You know, despite like body parts and whatever, right?'" Lin went on, "And I think that's the only time where it was nearly fetishized, but it's not. I don't think me being trans was the part that was fetishized as opposed to this is just how my body is, and he's not aware of what terms he should be using for a trans woman." Another interviewee, 23-year-old Emma, also recounted a story of how the word *gay* or the desires of gay men can work to delegitimize trans women's womanhood. "I get really anxious about the way that I'm being perceived. So, for gay men, I'm really scared sometimes that I'm just being perceived as a very feminine man when in fact that is not the case. I also get scared that I'm just like a femme boy situation when that is again not the case at all. I am a she, a woman," stated Emma, a white Latina working as a youth art instructor in Berkeley, California. "So yeah, I think it just makes me really anxious around gay men to be perceived as that," Emma further explained. "And gay men want men, and I'm not that. So, I think with straight men or just like men in general, I get fetishized a lot."

Sexual identities—or the language around sexual identities—can constrain and limit our understanding of bodies, gender, and desire. For instance, "gay" typically describes monosexual attraction—a man who desires other men or a woman who desires other women. A man calling sex with a trans woman "gay sex" can invalidate trans women and their womanhood. That is, in a cis society, where we understand gay identity as men who desire men, the term *gay* can partly work to fetishize and delegitimize trans women as just feminine men. As Lin suggested, this delegitimizing experience might be a case of the other person simply not being educated enough about trans people. Notably, Lin was in a polyamorous relationship with their sexual partner, and thus Lin might be more forgiving and more willing to do the labor of educating a partner compared to someone like Emma who was single and just looking for a hookup. The point being though: Language—particularly that around gender and sexuality—is constantly changing, and this language is powerful, whereby a lack of awareness can thwart comfort and pleasure. Moreover, certain sexual identities—such as the monosexual labels of gay and straight—may not fully capture desires for trans people or may not fully capture the complexities of gender and desire today. These experiences, though, around language and sexual identities shape experiences of comfort.

Comfort's Complexities

Like most things in life, comfort is complicated, and these complexities shape people's dating and sexual experiences. For instance, Carmen talked about the complexities of comfort in relation to trans for trans (t4t) relationships: "I could consider myself t4t at times, but I haven't allowed myself space to explore dating with other trans people. I did go on a date with someone who was trans feminine. And she had took me out on a picnic date which was nice. I think it was different just 'cause I used to think I couldn't be romantic with people who were also feminine." Carmen went on, "I think that I actually am really attracted to people who are effeminate. I think that it's more comforting if someone has a little bit of a feminine side to them." Carmen is open to trans masculine folks as well. As Carmen explained, "And I've gone on dates with trans masculine people, and I've shared romantic experiences, but not sexual yet. So, it's just, it's something I'm still exploring, but my preferences are open."

But despite this openness to t4t, cisness and compulsory heterosexuality still shape Carmen's comfort zone. "I think this goes back into trans dating, specifically t4t. I just need to step out of my comfort zone," Carmen explained. "I think I'm just very used to dating cis men. But I have given myself space to explore my emotional and romantic feelings with people who are also trans." Although Carmen finds comfort in dating cis men, Carmen finds a different type of comfort with other trans people. "It's scary, but in a way that I like it because I feel very comfortable. I think that it's just the fact that I'm with another trans individual who understands. We both share the very same experience," Carmen stated. "My struggles in that is just, it's that challenge of like going outside of my comfort zone and being able to not follow a cisheteronormative dating pool."

Like pleasure, comfort can be paradoxical. Larger social structures such as cisness and compulsory heterosexuality can shape how and why people may feel comfort in different contexts. There can be comfort in following dominant relationship models. Carmen even recognizes how cisness and compulsory heterosexuality influence the comfort Carmen finds in dating cis men. Indeed, within mainstream media and historically within the medical field, trans people are typically portrayed as heterosexual with a cis partner of the opposite gender.[41] There is supposed happiness and social acceptance in heterosexuality.[42] But even within this context, Carmen resists these restrictive norms by preferring bisexual or pansexual cis men rather than straight ones.

Comfort, though, can also disrupt and challenge dominant relationship structures. And t4t—as an example—can push back at cis heterosexual ways of dating. Carmen finds a different type of comfort in dating trans people—one of shared understanding. This t4t challenges the idea that trans people must date or partner with cis people. The comfort of t4t can also provide an alternative to the comfort zones of cisness and compulsory heterosexuality. Comfort can complicate comfort. And sometimes discomfort—especially going outside of our comfort zones—can lead to change, growth, and new forms of fulfillment.

Ultimately, comfort is complicated. We should not just assume that comfort is good or liberatory, as comfort is also shaped by power, society, historical contexts, and our social interactions. That is, like pleasure and joy—which people might derive from oppressing others, for instance—people might find comfort in following and upholding dominant structures in society, including those that oppress rather than liberate. "Comfort women," for example, were Asian women—mostly Korean—forced into sexual slavery by the Japanese armed forces during World War II. Around two hundred thousand Asian women were trafficked into "comfort stations" to keep soldiers from growing discontented during the war.[43] Comfort, in this instance, furthered the project of the nation and empire, while enacting racialized, gendered, and sexual harm on Asian women.[44] In this case, Japanese male soldiers' supposed need for "comfort" was used to justify enslavement and sexual violence.

We must, then, be critical of comfort. We must ask whose comfort we are centering and what the broader implications of that comfort are for all people involved. We should strive for comfort that liberates everyone, especially marginalized folks, from pain and suffering. We need comfort and pleasure that get us closer to freedom.

The Pleasurable Possibilities of Comfort

When I told friends and colleagues that I was writing a chapter about comfort, they were intrigued. Many agreed that comfort was an important aspect of their lives and building connection with others. And most folks felt that comfort was crucial and critical for many of their experiences of pleasure, including sexual pleasure. But they also said comfort isn't really sexy. How can a book about sex devote a whole chapter to comfort? Comfort might be a deeply important aspect of who we are and how we build relationships, but the concept isn't particularly seductive. Indeed, part of why comfort might be often overlooked in sexualities research is because it's not inherently seen as a sexual concept. Mothers comfort babies. We comfort our friends and family members when something tragic happens. But comfort can also be a critical element of fulfilling sexual relationships. It can be erotic, attractive, and orgasmic. It can be where that mind-blowing pleasure resides. And it can lead to great fucking sex.

Like many folks in this study, Chic found comfort (and great sex) in dating and hooking up with other trans folks. "A lot of people I have sex with are also trans feminine, nowadays, at least," Chic explained, "and they understood me being trans. If I had things to talk with them like, 'Oh, hey, I'm experiencing pleasure a little differently, so do this differently.' You know, discuss that kinda stuff." For Chic, who is white, t4t provided comfort in a shared understanding of being trans and in communicating one's pleasures. There is also comfort in Chic's own trans body that made recent sexual experiences really amazing. "In most of my sexual history, like pretransitioning, I've had some problems before during sex, like, enjoying sex, just getting off with other people," Chic detailed. "And despite some of the impediments that come with medically transitioning, like taking HRT [hormone replacement therapy] and stuff, I've been enjoying sex more than ever. I could get off with partners relatively a lot more easy than I was able to before. I just feel more comfortable. [. . .] Sex feels good now. Sex feels amazing now." Comfort with others and with one's self makes for better sex.

This comfort can also create space to explore more sexually. "Just exploring another person's body is a lot of fun," Chic explained. "Now more than ever, like, again, kinda how I like interacting sexually has changed since transitioning—I love just touching somebody all over, just seeing them, completely feeling them, and being felt." Chic further discussed the joys of sex and exploration. "Something that brings me a lot of joy during sex is being praised, just being told during a sexual interaction how hot I am or what somebody likes about me, like, 'Oh, your tits are so nice,' or like, 'Oh, your thighs are crazy,' or stuff like that." Chic continued: "Oh, something I love, it kinda goes hand-in-hand with exploring somebody's body, but finding the little things specifically that turn them on without them telling me. That's something I love doing." Getting even more specific, Chic stated, "And it's like, maybe it's a certain spot on their body that drives them crazy or maybe it's a particular way of talking to them or certain words and language that gets them going. It's fun." Comfort is fun. Comfort brings joy during sex. Comfort is hot.

Lately, Chic's great sex has been related to Patty—a white trans feminine person whom Chic was dating at the time of the interview. Chic lived in Pittsburgh, Pennsylvania, but met Patty in Atlanta, Georgia, at a furry convention—a place for "people who like to pretend to be [nonhuman] animals and hang out with each other," as Chic described it. In talking more about this current relationship with Patty, Chic discussed how comfort shapes their dating life, particularly one night when they went to a punk show together: "Being seen together, it was nice. We both got compliments from complete strangers. So getting to share that with her and kinda introduce her to that space. It was nice being comfortable together in public and being seen by other queer people as well." Chic went on to describe how this comfort led to a wonderful night, including respecting Patty's comfort zone. "It was just nice getting to have little moments like, 'Hey, let's do a shot together,' or considering going into the mosh pit. I wanted to go in the mosh pit. She didn't really want to. I was like, 'Okay, this is your first show. That's fine,'" Chic recounted. "It was a lot of fun getting to just share that time and space with her that night and just having these little transient interactions with random people, most of which I'll probably never see again, but just having those with her and getting to see little interactions she had with people. It was very nice." The comfort of being together in public, sharing little moments together, and respecting each other made for a very special night.

Chic also detailed one night when Chic and Patty had sex. "The night that we had together, she asked, at some point, closer to the beginning of when we were having sex, like, 'Hey, is there some title you'd like me to call you by, like Mistress or something?' And I was like, 'Oh, you know, Mistress, that's reserved for certain spaces.'" The comfort with Patty helped build communication. "And then she asked later on, 'Well, what about Mommy?' And I was like, 'We can try that.' And turns out, I really like it, and she ended up really liking it too," Chic recalled. "We both kinda discovered a lot about ourselves sexually that night. And I think that's so fun to do with just anybody during sex, having these discoveries, trying new things, and 'Oh, hey, this is really fun. Let's try this more. Let's explore.'"

This comfort shaped Chic's experiences of sexual exploration with Patty, including Chic performing sexually in unexpected ways. "I was able to have penetrative sex with her throughout that night. That was wild to me. And it was with somebody I just met. I was oozing with confidence that night. It was great." In addition to exploring erotic nicknames, Chic and Patty also explored other kinks, particularly when Chic discovered that Patty was into pup play—a kink in which people find sexual satisfaction and relaxation through taking on the role of dog or handler.[45] "I was like, 'Oh, really? That's cute.' And so that came up kinda organically when we were having sex. And I got my gear on me. I used to be a pup myself," Chic said, "so I had a leash and collar, and I pulled those out, and she actually brought her own too. We actually used her collar, which she had just worn all that day, and my leash." Chic went on to talk about this sexual exploration. "And I kinda helped her explore the puppy stuff more, and she kinda discovered that night that, 'Oh, hey, I really like pretending to be a dog for a while.' You know, you gotta lead her around on a leash and stuff, make her do some tricks, and make . . . it was really nice," Chic stated. Bringing it back to joy again, Chic said, "So that was an instance where I'd say I experienced that joy on a few levels, for sure. For sure, for sure. I mean, getting to explore her body, I found a lot of things that she likes without her telling me, like . . . it was great."

At this point in the interview, Chic was genuinely excited while recalling this amazing night with Patty. "Oh, one thing . . . oh, sorry. I'm excited talking about it now," Chic continued. "She was laying on the bed below me. I was over her, and I was fully hard, and she was semi-hard. She kinda has a smaller cock, even when fully erect, and I kinda pressed mine against her, and it turns out, oh, she's really into size comparison." Chic went on, "I didn't realize that. I just thought it was a hot thing to do at the time. I don't know. There were plenty of little moments that night like that where that sense of discovery and playfulness and fun just . . . it was really nice."

Comfort can be fun, hot, playful, exciting. Comfort can be a mode of relation that frees people to explore. Comfort can be where pleasure, liberation, and other possibilities reside. And as Chic's story also teaches us—and to which the next chapter turns—t4t might be where those possibilities reside too.

Comfort and the Paradox of Pleasure

4 t4t possibilities

I should have known that all roads would lead me back to Craigslist. Sort of.

This chapter is not *really* about Craigslist, but "t4t"—trans for trans—did start there.[1] You see, in the first two decades of the twenty-first century, Craigslist was a unique site for queer and trans people to find others for sex, dating, relationships, and hookups. As a young queer myself in the aughts, I sometimes found it difficult to find other people who desired feminine folks like me. But Craigslist provided a space where I could find and see trans women, trans femmes, and gender-expansive people being desired. Indeed, Craigslist's "casual encounters" page was a place one could find a variety of sexual fun with a plethora of people, and this section of the site included t4t—trans people seeking romantic and sexual encounters with each other. Unfortunately, these personal sections of Craigslist shut down in 2018 after the passage of FOSTA-SESTA—two "sex trafficking" bills that ended up harming a lot of online sexual spaces, particularly those for sex workers and queer and trans folks[2]—and as someone who used Craigslist and as someone who studied the m4m (men seeking men) section of the website,[3] I still mourn the loss of the "casual encounters" section of that website.[4] And so, while this chapter will show that trans people are still finding each other elsewhere, I want to acknowledge Craigslist—a hookup space, a sexual space, an erotic space—as the genesis of t4t.[5] Nowadays, t4t has morphed from its Craigslist beginnings into representing a trans politics of love and solidarity. For instance, t4t spaces, both online and in offline communities, often provide mutual aid, care, and support between and among trans people.[6] In finding community with other trans people, t4t makes life more livable, including for folks in this study.[7] t4t also decenters cisness. It provides recognition for trans people, especially that validation that cis society often withholds.[8] And t4t shows trans people that they deserve love and affirmation.

Building, then, on this Craigslist history as well as current t4t practices of love and solidarity, this chapter brings t4t back to its roots, exploring t4t as a site of romantic and sexual desire—a desire that also shapes trans identities, communities, and practices.[9] It also examines t4t as a dating and hookup strategy and documents t4t as a type of intimate relation building tactic. The chapter explores trans people dating each other, fucking each other, caring for each other, and affirming each other outside of cis society. Notably, while much scholarly work on t4t has come from the humanities and through examining cultural t4t productions such as novels, memoirs, art, blogs, and memes, this chapter builds on this rich literature to examine trans women's and femmes' personal experiences of t4t. In doing so, this chapter demonstrates how t4t can help us reimagine desire, dating, sex, and care. Indeed, t4t can make visible the importance of respect, communication, and connection in forming relationships and intimate bonds. It demonstrates how trans folks come to know themselves on their

t4t possibilities

own terms. And it exposes how cisness often shapes dating and hooking-up experiences. t4t reveals, then, how we can create new ways of intimately relating to one another, and it gives us strategies for getting to a better tomorrow.

Why Are All the Trans Folks Dating Each Other?

"I went on a date with a trans boi,"[10] 23-year-old Tiana began. "We went to a sushi bar, and they had just opened up a new side of the building—like they expanded—so we got to sit on the new side. And we sat there for like three and a half hours, and we had a great time. It was good. It was nice. It was really cute." Part of what made the date great was how the trans boi "treated me like a person," as Tiana explained. "They made me feel seen. I felt like our conversation was really genuine, and it made me laugh. They made me laugh a lot."

Mainstream media almost exclusively depicts trans folks dating cis people (if mainstream media even depicts trans folks at all, especially in romantic and intimate relationships). Moreover, the dominance of cisness, particularly within the medical field, constructs the "proper" trans subject as heterosexual and dating a cis person.[11] But a lot of trans folks aren't really into cis people, or, at least, not exclusively into cis people. Indeed, many trans people in this study, like Tiana, mostly dated other trans people. Larger cis society often obscures these t4t relationships; t4t, though, can tell us why trans folks might prefer dating other trans folks. It can also expose how cisness shapes dating, and what needs to change in order to make dating and relationships better for both trans and cis people alike.

For Tiana, this trans boi being funny met one of Tiana's key dating criteria. Indeed, Tiana, who was single and who was currently in a vet tech program in Alameda, California, typically dated people who were "normally trans or gender-nonconforming for the most part. They're normally not white. Everything else is pretty much a toss-up. I like people who are funny, but you don't have to necessarily be the most outgoing person to be funny." In reflecting on what made this sushi date memorable, Tiana said, "The conversation was so good, and I felt seen. They made me feel normal, and I know they respected me as a person. So, it was nice. That takes the cake for me. And I'm very simple. My version of a date is like a walk in the park, something simple like the sushi bar, nothing too extravagant because my goal is just to get to know that person."

t4t acknowledges and affirms trans people at the most fundamental level, before a relationship even begins. In a society that often invalidates trans people and trans lives, this affirmation both acknowledges trans people's humanity and challenges their devaluation. Trans folks can see and value other trans people on their own terms, not through the lens of cisness or compulsory heterosexuality.[12] Furthermore, trans people meeting and dating other trans people can help normalize dating and relationship experiences and disrupt cis ideas that construct trans people as abnormal, or that fetishize them, or that treat them as undesirable.[13] As Tiana's story reflects, t4t allows trans people to bypass many of the sex and dating concerns detailed in earlier chapters, and trans people can actually get to know each other as human beings. This ease, respect, and mutual recognition can allow for laughter, pleasure, joy, and fulfilling relationships.

Even so, Tiana gives us another glimpse into the potential problems and complications of t4t: race and racism. As a Black trans woman, Tiana preferred dating other trans or gender-nonconforming people of color. And many of the trans women and femmes of color in this study discussed wanting to date people of a similar racial or ethnic background. As 20-year-old Nour—a single, full-time student living in Claremont, California—explained, "Last year, it was the first time I heard about t4t. And I'm like, that makes so much sense—that kind of community aspect. And I got to meet another trans Egyptian person, who also came from a really religious Muslim background." Meeting someone also trans and also Egyptian was a profound experience for Nour: "And that was the first time that's ever happened, so that felt really, really healing too. And yeah, I think that's like a big thing about what I look for in a person."

Trans people, like any group of people, are not a monolith. The idea of t4t, though, often privileges trans identity and experiences over others, such as race, class, or religion. That is, t4t might implicitly privilege whiteness as it focuses on trans identity over racial and other identities in thinking about connection and community. But racism within queer and trans communities can make connecting with white trans people its own form of labor for trans people of color.[14] To avoid this intimate and emotional labor, trans people of color may selectively date other trans people of color. In other words, a Black trans person may date another Black trans person to avoid dealing with *both* racial and trans fetishizing within a relationship. This selectivity mitigates the effects of whiteness *and* cisness within intimate and romantic relationships. And while these personal choices may not transform larger structural inequalities, such as white supremacy and trans-antagonism, this dating strategy does allow trans people of color to find respite—or even healing—with one another.[15] Importantly, this respite can be crucial in a world where trans people of color face disproportionate rates of violence, including murder, for being who they are.[16]

So why are trans folks dating each other? Because it helps trans people affirm one another outside of cis fetishization, objectification, and invalidation. Trans people can get to know one another on a foundation of mutual recognition. And this recognition through t4t shows the importance of affirmation and respect in building relationships. But t4t might also have a whiteness problem, as race, class, religion, and other intersecting identities and experiences can muddle t4t relationships that often prioritize trans identity over other identities. t4t—like most things in life—is complicated.

Staying Safe and Avoiding Transmisogyny

In addition to affirmation and recognition, trans folks also seek out other trans folks as a way to actively avoid discrimination and to maintain physical safety. In discussing dating cis folks, especially dating "hetero cisgender men," Tiana stated, "I have to deal with transphobia from people who are attracted to trans people. And it's weird. It's very weird. There's also a level of misogyny that's happening because, again, those roles that they would normally put on a cisgender woman, they put onto me." Tiana went on to detail this harassment and misogyny. "I have to be the romantic one. Or aggressiveness, when I'm not interested, is also something that's like really new for me because when I was a cisgender man, that wasn't anything I had to deal with," Tiana explained. "But [dating as a woman] there's that misogyny thing where it's like, 'No, you're property, and if you don't wanna date me, why not?' And they get upset." Tiana further elucidated how trans women experience this misogyny in particular ways. "But me being a trans woman, they have this level of like, 'You should be grateful that I'm attracted to you. You should be grateful that I'm messaging you and blah, blah,

blah,'" exclaimed Tiana. "So when you ignore those people or tell them, 'I'm not interested,' the aggression that jumps out is so strong. So, safety is always my number one concern."

Avoiding discrimination. Staying safe. Not dealing with misogyny and transphobia (i.e., not dealing with transmisogyny). These strategies are also partly why trans folks turn to or prefer t4t. Indeed, trans people often navigate safety concerns and violence when dating.[17] And this fear is not unwarranted. Studies have shown that trans people, especially trans people of color, experience gender-based and intimate partner violence at significantly higher rates than the general population.[18] Many trans people in this study discussed fearing for their safety, including the potential of being violently attacked or murdered, as a major concern when navigating dating and hookups. As 30-year-old Bella, who lived in Memphis, Tennessee, stated, "If they are trans, then there's less vetting sometimes, or a lot of the time." With cis people, there is more vetting. "I gotta make sure I'm not gonna like die. I need to make sure their understanding of trans stuff. I'm there to date. I'm not there to like be someone's teacher," Bella explained. "There's red flags I look out for. Some less obvious than others." Bella, who is white and who was in two relationships during the time of the study, went on to give a specific example. "I guess a less obvious one is if someone puts together trans women and then femme guys in the same sentence, that's a huge red flag," Bella detailed. "Because one, I don't know why they're sitting there in that same category. And two, you're gonna be gravely disappointed because I'm not and we're not. And it's just, they don't even get out what they think they're gonna get if they expect femme guy."

Masculine aggressiveness is often about heterosexuality and its link to misogyny. That is, part of heterosexuality is the "misogyny paradox"—that men devalue women and femininity, and yet, also supposedly love women. Heterosexuality also eroticizes the gender binary, including feminine subordination and masculine domination.[19] Tiana's story reflects a similar and related transmisogyny paradox—certain cis hetero men desire trans women, but some find shame in this desire and may be transphobic.[20] Some men also respond with aggressiveness, feeling that trans women should be thankful for cis men's attention. But trans women, like all women, are devalued and subordinated through these misogynistic behaviors. Tiana even noted how Tiana did not experience this aggressiveness from men before transitioning—it is about subordinating women. Indeed, harassment in dating relationships is often a prime place for men to assert their masculine dominance over women.[21] And transmisogyny, like misogyny, shapes dating—especially heterosexual dating—experiences.[22]

Navigating this potential for violence requires labor from trans women and femmes to engage in vetting strategies when dating and hooking up with cis people. One reason cis men, in particular, may commit violence against trans women is because of the dehumanization, objectification, and fetishization that characterizes some cis men's attraction to trans women.[23] Some cis men may also lump trans women in with femme guys, as Bella noted, which delegitimizes trans women's womanhood. It should go without saying, at this point in the book, that trans women are not feminine men. But the tendency of cis men to lump trans women and feminine men together constructs them as merely sexual objects in service of these men's own pleasure. In turn, trans women and femmes have to vet their potential dating partners, and trans women and femmes of color may have to use even more vetting tactics to avoid both racial and trans fetishization.[24]

A response to these safety concerns is t4t. Similar to lesbian separatism, t4t can be an escape from misogyny and discrimination. Indeed, a sect of lesbian separatists built political futures on the belief that heterosexuality puts women in too close contact with their oppressors—men.[25] Separating from men by choosing lesbianism, then, could challenge the patriarchy and its reinforcement through heterosexuality. t4t meets a similar need by allowing trans people to feel safe and seen and by challenging cisness and compulsory heterosexuality as foundational to how people have to interact romantically, sexually, or intimately.

Importantly, though, lesbian separatism has been critiqued for being gender essentialist. Men are not inherently oppressive. And women of color may need to form political coalitions with men of color to challenge white supremacy and other structures of oppression.[26] Moreover, cis people are also not inherently oppressive. And trans people deserve to be loved and desired by cis people too.[27] Separatism may not work, then, for all trans people, including trans people in more rural or isolated areas who may not be able to only separate with other trans people. Trans separatism might be an individual strategy for some to avoid danger, but ultimately, we need to change the larger society to end transmisogyny and make the world safe for all. t4t exposes, then, the safety needs and concerns of trans people, but it can't be the only solution to addressing these problems.

Freedom from Fetishization and Heterosexual Cisness

Besides dating, Tiana also discussed t4t in relation to sex and hooking up. "I'm not really big on hooking up and the majority of the reason is because of some of the ugly experiences I've had. Some dudes will be really sweet to you on the apps that you're on, and then you get to them and they're pushy," Tiana explained. "Or there's just an expectation because they'll ask you to come hang out and then you get there and it's like, 'If we're not having sex, this isn't gonna happen.' So, yeah, it's just one of those things where it's like you turn into an object." In comparison, Tiana discussed a hookup with someone who was "exploring their gender." "If it's with someone I'm comfortable with, I like being able to provide a space for someone else to feel that freedom. And it's just a very human thing. It's a very human thing," Tiana stated. "And when I get to engage in human behavior and I'm not being fetishized and I'm not feeling like an object, I feel free. I feel comfortable and I know that person feels the same way. It's very rewarding." Like Carmen in the last chapter, Tiana described how this hookup made Tiana feel comfortable and respected. "They saw me as another human being, and they respected me," Tiana said. "They respected my wishes, and I respected theirs. And I think it was a very healing moment for them as well, being that they were struggling with their identity at the time."

In addition to affirmation and safety, t4t can be an escape from the hypersexualization, objectification, and fetishization that trans people may experience with certain cis folks, especially sexually. Trans women of color such as Tiana have to navigate racial and trans fetishization,[28] whereby avoiding these gender and racial stereotypes altogether can be freeing and healing. Indeed, t4t can be a way to heal from the trauma of living in a cis society,[29] and comfort and respect are foundational to these experiences. Tiana also saw t4t as potentially helping the other person who was exploring their gender and struggling with their identity. In loving another trans body, one can learn to love their own trans body, and this love and affirmation can be liberating.

At the end of the interview, when asked if there was anything else Tiana wanted to mention, Tiana said, "Maybe asking people if they've had an experience dating someone else trans and did that make them feel safe or how was that experience for them because there's kind of a movement within the trans community right now, t4t." Tiana went on to discuss how dominant notions of gender and sexuality can shape people's dating lives and how t4t can challenge and disrupt cis ways of thinking, doing, and being. "Trans people obviously, we're pretty open-minded about gender identity," Tiana explained. "So I didn't realize how deeply I had fell into heteronormative things—like, I'm a feminine person, so I have to date someone who's a masculine person. And I had to unpack that around the time I even came out as trans." Tiana continued, "Literally, I don't have the same problems. I still do because I still deal with people. I still am attracted to and date people who are cisgender. And even trans people fall into heteronormative things. But t4t has opened my eyes up about a lot of things, and it's made me feel more normal in a way."

t4t, which Tiana called "a movement," has the power to disrupt cisness and compulsory heterosexuality—to collectively challenge dominant ideologies—even on personal and intimate levels. For instance, t4t allowed Tiana to question Tiana's own cis ways of thinking about gender, sexuality, and relationship dynamics; it reshaped Tiana's thinking about womanhood, about dating, and about what it means to be feminine or masculine. t4t also challenges the notion that trans people only date cis people. Trans people can find value outside of cisness, as t4t centers trans people, their pleasures, and their desires. t4t also bases connections, including intimate connections, on mutual love, support, respect, comfort, connection, communication, and solidarity.[30] In doing so, t4t provides alternative avenues to building relationships outside of heterosexual cisness.

Like Two Veterans Sharing Our Scars: On Similarity

In addition to affirmation, respect, safety, and freedom from fetishization and gender stereotypes, part of t4t is also built on notions of shared experiences and similarity. "There was still that layer of understanding because we're both trans feminine, and we come from a very similar place of realizing it late in life and having to contend with all the same things and having the same medical journeys and stuff," explained 30-year-old Monica, who worked in management and lived in Thousand Oaks, California. "And so, talking about that stuff came very naturally, whereas talking about medical stuff to literally anybody else can feel a little bit invasive. But for us it was like two veterans sharing our scars." Later in the interview, Monica, who is white, discussed currently dating and being in a relationship with a gender-fluid person who previously identified as trans masculine. "I have similar experience with him, as far as knowing, understanding, and feeling the same things," Monica stated. "Just we're coming from the opposite end of a spectrum but our experiences are still very similar. And we just clicked so well when we got to know each other that we both feel like home is wherever we are together."

Homophily is the concept that people often date similar others—birds of a feather flock together.[31] Homophily, though, can maintain social hierarchies, such as when white people only want to date or friend other white people or cis people only want to date or friend other cis people. But for marginalized folks, homophily can be a way to avoid discrimination such as trans people not wanting to deal with cis people's antitrans biases or stereotypes. Another reason trans people may date other trans people is just the potential ease of understanding each other. This shared connection makes for less labor—less effort compared to educating cis people, fewer invasive questions about medical histories and gender. There is an ease, then, in this mutual understanding, in not having to explain the trans experience. There is a feeling of home in feeling similar things.

Importantly, while race may complicate notions of t4t similarity (as discussed earlier), gender does not seem to. That is, among the trans women and femmes interviewed for this book, there doesn't seem to be a need for a shared gender experience within t4t relations. Like Tiana, for Monica, t4t doesn't always mean trans femme for trans femme. And even if trans folks come "from the opposite end of the spectrum"—as Monica said about currently dating a gender-fluid person—trans people know and understand the trans journey. t4t challenges, then, this cis idea that men and women or masculine and feminine people are "opposites" who can't understand each other. That is, within cis heterosexual relationships, men and women are often seen as complete opposites (men are from Mars and women are from Venus), even though they are supposed to love and desire one another.[32] This idea of gender difference does not seem to carry much weight within t4t relationships, as many of the trans people in this study never saw a trans person of a different gender as dissimilar to them. In this regard, t4t becomes a form of relationality that challenges how compulsory heterosexuality and cisness often shape dating, gender, sex, and relationships. t4t builds a world beyond gender difference, where masculine and feminine people and trans folks across the gender spectrum can all connect, love, respect, and support one another. In doing so, t4t challenges and expands ideas of gender.

Gender Exploration

t4t can also allow for an expansion of gender and identity. For example, Emily, who in the last chapter talked about bottoming and topping as a trans person, also discussed how t4t shaped gender exploration. "For a long time when I was getting in as a cis man, I didn't really know what transgender was completely. I never really had a trans person that I was very close with," Emily explained. "So it was difficult for me to even sexually get into the idea of, 'Oh, this is a woman with a penis,' because of the fact, I think, maybe it was something to do with gender dysphoria, because I thought, I can't really be trans feminine unless I was actually a woman." Emily continued: "But then, the first person I had sex with was at the time, they identified as trans feminine, and it was really kind of shocking to me. I was still cis. And then even after we broke up, it was very devastating for me. But it kind of opened a door of like trans femmes being a possibility." This encounter opened up Emily's ideas about gender and transness in a way that was "very freeing," as Emily realized trans folks didn't have to have binary identities, but they could embrace gender expansiveness or androgyny. As Emily explained, "There's many different gender identities, and I think transgender is very freeing. I personally love freedom as a principle."

Sex with another trans person can expand ideas about gender, which can be freeing. Under cisness, there are only the binary concepts of men and women, and this gender binary shapes transness as well. Indeed, the gender binary often privileges traditionally masculine trans men and traditionally feminine trans women over other expressions of trans identity.[33] As dominant ideas of gender are also bound up with race, white trans people are also privileged within this binary.[34] But this binary can obscure other ways of being free and embodying gender within this world.

For Emily, the possibility of being trans feminine without being a woman did not exist until Emily had sex with a trans feminine person. Since trans people don't typically grow up around other trans people, the erotic, for Emily, became a site of learning about and producing gender, identity, and transness. Indeed, through attraction to a trans person, someone may see themselves in the trans person they are attracted to. Sex itself—including t4t sex—can be crucial for identity formation and development.[35] And t4t sex can allow for exploration of gender and bodies that feels affirming, safe, and satisfying.[36] The erotic, including t4t desires, can expand gender possibilities.

Pitfalls and Complications

Despite its liberatory potential, t4t is not without problems. Not without assault. Not without danger. That is, shared identities and presumed similarities do not inherently keep us safe. While t4t can be a strategy to avoid cis violence and find safety and respite from cis society, trans people can do harm as well. For example, while Monica discussed feeling "like home" within a current t4t relationship, with one trans feminine person Monica previously dated this feeling of home was definitely not the case. As Monica explained, "Sexual discussion with them always led around to genitalia-focused things—a specific phrase that I can think of is 'Thank God you still have a cock,' which is really gross. I mean, yes, while I am now presently comfortable with it, that was not something I wanted to hear at that time." Monica went on, "It was like a skin-crawling moment. And I just felt like, 'How can this person be part of the same community as me but lack all of this empathy that I have?'" Bella, who talked about vetting strategies with cis people, even discussed being sexually assaulted by another trans person. As Bella explained, "I had a situation where I got sexually assaulted by someone who's trans masc. And even queer cis women weren't really listening. And that's because of transmisogynistic ideas, like being socialized male or something, that there was just no way I could have dealt with that."

Trans people can enact violence, and t4t spaces and relationships are not inherently safe.[37] That is, trans people are people, which means they are also capable of hurting and harming others, including other trans people. And intracommunity violence—including sexual assault, as Bella discussed—is real. Moreover, because trans people face discrimination and abuse in medical settings and within other institutions in society, they may be less likely to seek medical care or other support after an assault,[38] and they might not want to expose other trans people for committing this violence. The fear of hurting the community can lead to silence around t4t violence.[39] Furthermore, essentialist notions of gender can also work to delegitimize this violence. According to Bella, some queer cis women did not even believe that a trans masculine person could assault a trans woman. This logic presumes that trans women aren't women (or were "socialized male") and cannot experience sexual assault—or at least cannot experience sexual assault from trans men and from trans masculine folks. These gender-essentialist ideas are transmisogynistic—as they deny trans women their womanhood—and these ideas obscure t4t violence.

t4t possibilities

Moreover, like race, class, religion, and other social categories, sexual identities can also thwart t4t connection and lead to painful experiences with other trans folks. Emily discussed a bad experience with a trans person who was deeply invested in her own sexual identity. "The trans woman that I dated, I was telling her, 'Hey, I feel kind of fluid about my gender. Would that be a problem for you?' And she said, 'Yeah, because I'm gay. I like women or feminine people, specifically,'" Emily recounted. "She was understanding that I needed to figure my stuff out, but it did seem like her preferences were kind of set like, 'No, I date strictly like feminine people.'" After they broke up, Emily felt "some relief because I felt like, 'Oh, wow, okay, I can finally express my fluidity or just my gender freely.'" These experiences, though, have shaped Emily's gender struggles. "One challenge is sort of just having anxiety about presentation," Emily explained. "Am I feminine enough? Will dressing masculine make me feel invalid of my trans identity and people will start assuming I'm cisgender because of it? Just stuff like that."

While Emily found freedom and gender exploration through t4t (as discussed in the previous section), Emily's gender fluidity did not align with how this trans woman saw her sexual identity, and hence, the relationship didn't work. In the last chapter, we saw how sexual identity can thwart relationships between cis and trans folks. Similarly, a gay identity, or sexual identities more broadly, can thwart connection among trans women and femmes, as dominant monosexual identities such as gay and straight often exclude gender fluidity and desire for fluid or nonbinary people.[40] The ending of the relationship provided some freedom for Emily to continue exploring the expansive possibilities of gender. At the same time, the relationship caused Emily more anxiety over Emily's own gender identity and presentation.

These gendered anxieties—which stem from the broader dominance of cisness and compulsory heterosexuality that this book is about—can shape sexual encounters, even with another trans person. "The last time was with a trans woman," Emily recalled. "We didn't go all the way in terms of like penetration, but she did give me a hand job. We even engaged in somewhat kinky activities like spanking and stuff." Emily found the encounter "very exhilarating and fun," but it also led to "a weird feeling though about my gender because I kind of had feelings that maybe I was the cis man in the relationship, that maybe I was the guy in a relationship because I'm just used to that. Like, should I have a beard to express that? That was the thought that came across my mind even though I was wearing a wig, I had makeup on, I was very feminine." Emily continued, "I felt like we were one in that moment, and, in some ways, made me comfortable being trans. But in another point, it made me kind of like question what I was wearing, because, again, I was kind of thinking, 'Is this my right gender in this form?'" Emily further contemplated the influence of compulsory heterosexuality in this context: "I wonder if it's also because we normalize relationships where it's a man and a woman, a masculine and a feminine person. But I was kind of like, 'Should I be the masculine person in this relationship instead of being androgynous or feminine?'"

Being one with this trans person, Emily felt comfortable being trans. Simultaneously, though, because cis society constructs relationships in binary, heterosexual terms, Emily experienced gender anxiety. Despite presenting in traditionally feminine ways—makeup, a wig, not having a beard—Emily still felt like a cis man. Under cisness, only a cis masculine man and a cis feminine woman should be having sex; for trans people, this dynamic often translates to a masculine man having sex with a traditionally feminine

t4t possibilities [89]

trans woman. In this context, then, two femmes having sexual encounters together seems abnormal, or even impossible. As cisness obscures t4t, some trans people may not even be able to think outside the gender binary when hooking up with another trans person. Cisness, then, thwarts gender possibilities and pleasure and shapes the intimate in such a powerful way that some trans people may still question their gender while having t4t sex; as we've established, t4t is complicated.

The Pleasurable Possibilities of t4t

Similar to the ending of the last chapter—where I discussed how comfort can be sexy and lead to great pleasure—t4t can also be quite erotic. For instance, t4t often centers trans pleasure. And in centering trans desires, including trans sexual desires for other trans people, t4t can challenge sexual cissexism—a process that dehumanizes and objectifies trans women and femmes. t4t can also deeply affirm trans people and their gender. And this affirmation can be orgasmic. t4t, then, can be where great sex and pleasure reside.

Indeed, 37-year-old Dakota—a white nurse residing in Seattle, Washington—discussed how a sexual connection with another trans person brings a special type of pleasure that can challenge the fetishization of trans people. "I'm pan, but I tend to lean towards femmes, and I heavily lean towards trans femmes," explained Dakota. "It's easy. I don't have to explain things to trans femmes. I feel like there's an automatic connection on a deeper level." Dakota, who was seeing someone during the time of the interview but didn't want to label the relationship, went on to talk about a recent hookup with a trans woman. "Neither of us have had bottom surgery, and there's an element of that that was really special," Dakota stated. "I don't know how else to say it. Like having a similar body type in that sense of recognizing, 'Yeah, I know what feels good for me, and I know that this is okay,' and we're both very good at communicating what we want in the moment. [. . .] It felt very much like we could connect on a deeper level than a lot of my hookups have been." For Dakota, the "passion level was really high" during this hookup because both trans women saw each other as humans, "but without us being fetishes for each other, because there wasn't that. It was just us existing as two trans women getting to be with each other and feeling like it was normal, if that makes sense." Dakota went on, "Now you get to feel like a whole human when you're dating another trans woman. It's how it feels for me, at least. When you're hooking up with another trans woman, you just feel like you're just seen as a human, not as anything to explore."

Dakota also contrasted t4t hookups with a bad sexual experience with a cis man. "So right after I got divorced, I tried to hook up with a dude, and it was awful. It was really bad. Because they wanted to fuck me, but they wanted to avoid my body parts. They wanted to avoid my penis," Dakota recalled. "It felt very fetishy because of that, like, I was checking off a list for them, kind of, it felt like. And so, I stopped halfway through because I was like, 'I'm done with this. This is not working for me.' Because I want to be looked at as a whole human. So that's really a learning experience for me." Dakota continued: "I had talked to them on the apps, and they were interested in me, but then when it got to me in person, it became very fetishy. And very gross. Because it felt nice to be wanted, but then I realized what they wanted was just the experience and not really me. It was a really gross moment."

The erotic possibilities of t4t can challenge the sexual cissexism that thwarts pleasure for trans people. That is, t4t experiences can challenge the dehumanization processes that trans people are something "to explore," as Dakota stated. Indeed, as documented in chapter 2, a form of sexual cissexism is how some cis people objectify and fetishize trans people.[41] For Dakota, it was nice to feel desired by a cis man, but it became clear that this man was only interested in exploring for his own sexual pleasure. He did not desire Dakota as a person. Dakota resisted by ending the sexual encounter—and, ultimately, by turning to t4t.

For Dakota, t4t—especially the connection with another trans woman and having similar body types—allowed for greater intimacy and erotic possibilities. t4t, then, creates space for passion, which, along with good communication, leads to pleasure rather than unwanted objectification. Notably, t4t is not only about community and social support, but includes how trans pleasure, trans desires, and t4t sex can do the important work of challenging sexual cissexism.[42] In challenging this fetishization and objectification of trans people, t4t allows for pleasure to actually flourish.

Going on, Dakota further described the beauty of t4t in relation to sex, bodies, and pleasure. "I'm obviously trans, when you look at me, it's not a question that comes up as easily. It's more of the question of what's going on underneath my clothes. Because that can be like a little bit more of the element of how do we interact physically?" For Dakota, these questions often carry less significance within t4t relationships. "I found that [. . .] when I'm hooking up with other trans women, it's not as much of a conversation," Dakota stated. "I've had friends that've had bottom surgery and friends that haven't. And we didn't know until our clothes were off, and we just went with it. And I think that's really beautiful."

These moments are partly meaningful because Dakota still has bodily concerns. "I think I'm worried that I won't be enough. I think I'm worried that they won't enjoy what's underneath my clothes," Dakota explained. "Being trans and being on HRT [hormone replacement therapy] obviously changes your physical body, but also changes, like, if you have a penis, it changes your penis, obviously, to where it's a little bit different than a lot of penises, or cis male penises. Trans woman penises, or 'girl dick' as I call it, is a little bit different." Dakota went on to delineate this difference. "Some girls lose their ability to use it at all and some still have it. And often, it's smaller or different and works different and feels different and different things come out. And so, if you're used to another type of penis, it can be a bit of a journey. And that isn't always received super well." This bodily difference and people not potentially knowing or understanding it can create some anxiety. As Dakota further explained, "So I'm a little bit nervous about that when it happens. Like, is this gonna be a good thing? That's the reason I like hooking up with trans girls." With other trans women, there can be a shared sexual understanding of the trans body. "We know, we remember even if we don't have a penis anymore, we remember what it looked like, remember what it was, remember how it was to have that when you first transitioned. And it doesn't feel invalidating," Dakota explained.

Like Carmen in the last chapter, Dakota troubles the notion of all bodies being the same. "Girl dick," in this instance, references how penises can be different and how we may need more expansive language to discuss genitals beyond the categories provided by cis understandings of sex, gender, and bodies. Dakota's use of "girl dick" is not meant to fetishize trans women and femmes, but to acknowledge how medical transitioning can affect trans people's bodies. Trans women on HRT do not have the same bodies as cis men, as transition can lead to changes in desires, arousal, sensitivity of sex organs, and orgasms.[43] Notably, within the dominant medical framing of trans people and dysphoria, trans people are not supposed to enjoy their genitals.[44] "Girl dick" becomes a way, then, to decouple body parts from gender and shows how genitals can be sites of erotic trans pleasure.[45]

Dakota's story, though, also exposes how within the larger society we lack representation and education around not only trans bodies but also t4t intimacy. In turn, cisness and compulsory heterosexuality often shape how many people think about and view sex. But what sexual and intimate possibilities can emerge from t4t? One possibility is a world, including a sexual world, less centered on genitals.[46] For Dakota, genitals don't matter in t4t encounters. Both partners communicate and go with the flow, and interacting physically is about mutual pleasure. Notably, many cis people don't understand trans bodies, which creates anxiety for Dakota. But trans folks start with a more shared understanding of the body, including of genitals and pleasure, which can lead to more satisfying hookups and sex. In turn, this pleasure, this satisfaction, this understanding can be beautiful—can be validating.

Additionally, Dakota discussed t4t sex in relation to communication, care, and bodily pleasure. "I'm a really touchy, feely human, so like, really love languages are feelings. I like everything from head to toe, basically. All of the things that feel like rubbing or scratching or kissing or pulling or choking or any of that. Fantastic. Biting. Yeah. Go for it," Dakota stated. "But I love blowjobs and anal and all the things that are like that. I wouldn't say I'm really kinky, but I am into the full experience." For Dakota, though, it's essential to have conversations before the encounter. "I've been with people that are not [into the full experience], and that's like, can be a challenge to figure out, like if you're not feeling good. Like I know I've had trans girls that just don't like their penis and don't want it touched and so we just avoid it," Dakota explained. "But those are usually talked about in the process of like, because they're pretty open about it if they don't feel good about it. But I would love . . . I love doing both. Like I will give head, and they can give head. Great. We can both do anal. Great. Let's take turns. We can do all sorts of things."

Sexual communication often correlates with sexual satisfaction.[47] And talking to and checking in with a partner can be really sexy. For some trans people, this sexual communication can also be about their body or genitals, and in t4t encounters, there can be a deeper understanding and respect for another trans person's potential dysphoria. Someone asking how to refer to or engage with another person's genitals—without being hung up on them—can also be erotic. As trans women are often reduced to sexual objects,[48] this communication and checking in can challenge cisness and sexual cissexism, as care and communication center trans pleasure and trans people's needs. t4t can provide a space where this communication and care are more prominent, whereby asking about genitals isn't invasive but is about respect and pleasure.

t4t sex can also be orgasmic and gender-affirming. Discussing the person Dakota is currently seeing, Dakota said, "When you transition, you start to feel orgasms differently. The feel becomes more full body, and when your dick doesn't get hard the same way, things transition. So, it's the very best blowjob I've ever had in my life because I didn't feel like a guy. I felt like a woman." This orgasmic moment shaped Dakota's feelings of being complete: "I screamed a lot. It was very, very intimate. It was very, very special.

There was a lot of knowing what they were doing. They really knew what they were doing for me and had asked all the right questions and had tried all the right things, and learned from it." Dakota went on, "So I think it really, I don't know how to say it except for just, it was really like, oh, this is what it feels like when it's done right. This is what it's like to have . . . This is what, like, when I feel complete, and it feels complete, this is what that feels like. Got it. This is what I've been missing."

Trans people going through gender-affirming hormone therapy can experience orgasms in new locations and have longer and multiple-peak orgasms. Gender-affirming hormone therapy can positively improve orgasms, then, for people going through medical gender transition.[49] Dakota relates these new feelings of orgasms to gender affirmation—to feeling "like a woman." Dakota's experience of orgasming reconfigures womanhood as not about the absence of a penis, but potentially about a different experience of the penis and pleasure. Notably, though, this pleasure and affirmation happened within a particular context—t4t. That is, Dakota related this pleasure and affirmation to the other trans person's knowing what they were doing, communicating, and listening and learning. Through this sexual communication, orgasmic pleasure, and gender affirmation, Dakota felt complete.

Through Dakota's story, we can see the pleasurable possibilities of t4t when we take it back to its Craigslist roots—of t4t being about trans sexual relations with other trans people. t4t pleasure, including sexual pleasure, can challenge the sexual cissexism, fetishization, and dehumanization that trans people often face in sexual encounters. Moreover, as pleasure is a measure of freedom, t4t also shows how centering trans pleasure can challenge the pleasure deficit that many trans people may experience. While sexual cissexism—and cisness more broadly—can thwart pleasure, t4t both expands ideas of pleasure (such as away from genitals) and shows how care and connection can help cultivate it. t4t also reveals how trans sexual pleasure can be gender affirming. t4t, including t4t sex, can make life livable. It can make trans folks feel complete. t4t relationships, then, that center affirmation, safety, care, and communication can lead to good sex, great dates, orgasmic pleasure, and fuller human experiences. These are the world-building strategies that we all should take from t4t to work toward a better tomorrow.

5 *Gender Liberation and the Abolition of Sexual Identities*

"I think transmisogyny gets written into basically every part of society—at least in the U.S.—probably other places," stated 36-year-old Delilah. "I just kind of think everyone comes with it built-in, and if you don't take it out, that is just how you feel." On a Zoom call from Minneapolis, Minnesota, Delilah went on to discuss how to address transmisogyny—the intersection of transphobia and misogyny. As Delilah explained, "But you know, people being less concerned about what junk a person has would be a great start. And not directly tying that to what someone's sexual orientation is."

Delilah explicitly links transmisogyny to people's obsession with genitals and the tying of genitals to sexual orientation. Indeed, a major culprit in sustaining myths about the naturalness of heterosexuality and the gender binary is the continued cultural dominance of fixed sexual identities focused on gender and genitals. In the now canonical *Epistemology of the Closet*, queer theorist Eve Sedgwick noted how sexuality encompasses a range of desires, behaviors, acts, and attractions.[1] People desire various physical characteristics, including race, body size, age, height, and other features. People like engaging in different sex acts, from penile-vaginal sex to masturbation to oral to anal to anything your mind can think of. People also have a variety of erotic zones and sensations from the neck to the ear to the breasts to the feet. People vary too in terms of sex drive, from not wanting sex at all to wanting sex all the time. And people differ in the number of partners they want during sex, from solo or one partner to an orgy. The list can go on and on, with the point being: Sexuality encompasses so much more than just gender and genitals. So how did gender and genitals become *the* main ways to label our desires through the idea of sexual orientation?[2]

To partly answer this question, academics often turn to philosopher and historian Michel Foucault. As documented in Foucault's *The History of Sexuality*, and as discussed in chapter 2 of this book, the categories of heterosexuality and homosexuality were invented in the late nineteenth century.[3] Western societies, in seeking to control populations and compel them to reproduce, created heterosexuality as the norm.[4] Simultaneously, they constructed homosexuality as "perverse" to scare and discipline people into conformity.[5] Of course, before the invention of sexual identities, people engaged in same-sex relations, but those behaviors were not tied to an identity. In other words, people didn't necessarily think that same-sex desires or same-sex sexual behaviors revealed some inner truth about who they were. But by the early twentieth century, people began accepting the idea that their desires—and specifically their gender and genital desires—defined who they were as people, that their gender and genital desires determined their identities.

Importantly, the sedimentation of sexual identities as a main way of organizing society happened over time and did not just happen in the clinic or in scientific journals.[6] For instance, through industrialization and through people moving away from their families and to cities, folks could form communities with others who shared similar same-sex desires.⁷ These urban gay subcultures that formed in the early twentieth century helped to birth and gave meaning to the category of the homosexual.⁸ Then, during the Cold War era, the state began taking a particular invested interest in people classified as homosexual, especially in constructing them as deviant. For example, homosexuality got linked to communism (or the idea that gay people could be easily bribed by communists), and thus gay and lesbian people were seen as a threat to national security and were expelled from the federal government.⁹ Around the same time, legislators, judges, immigration officials, and military personnel began passing laws restricting homosexuals from various facets of life, such as from joining the military and from immigrating to the United States. Homosexuality became not only a medical category or community identity but also a legal category.¹⁰ And while the term was often used within dominant society to pathologize gay people, folks rallied behind the category of homosexual to form political actions such as getting homosexuality removed from the *DSM* as a mental illness in 1973. A decade later, during the AIDS crisis, new political coalitions formed, whereby gay, lesbian, bisexual, and trans people as well as other groups of people such as drug users and sex workers came together to fight back against the government's inactions around HIV/AIDS.¹¹ Partly from these political actions, such as from the activist group Queer Nation, *queer* got reclaimed as an umbrella term to capture this more expansive politics and coalitional work. Homosexuality (and heterosexuality) are very recent categories, formations, and creations. And the history of sexual identities is largely about controlling us and disciplining our desires in service of maintaining compulsory heterosexuality.¹² We do not have to organize society this way.

Furthermore—and the heart of the argument of this chapter—sexual identities, especially monosexual sexual identities, often focus on just gender attraction and can maintain the myth that gender is fixed, inherent, and natural.[13] Let's consider "gay" identity, for example. If gay identity hinges on the notion that one is a man inherently attracted to other men, then it assumes there is a biological category of "man." That is, if you believe you are inherently attracted to men, then you have to believe there is something biologically essential about the category "man" to which you are attracted. In reality, however, the category and meaning of "man," and related ideas of manhood, have varied throughout time, across cultures and contexts, and in intersection with other social categories such as race and ability that shape its meaning.[14] But through our culture's investment in sexual identities, gender attraction gets privileged over all other types of attraction, and gender categories can get reified as inherent and immutable.[15] Sexual identities, then, maintain gender essentialism.[16] Or, in other words, using identity as a core way of organizing sexuality in society maintains cisness and prevents liberation.

This final chapter wrestles with the complexities of sexual identity, ultimately calling for their abolition. Yes, I know identity can be important—life-savingly important—to finding and building community, especially with similarly marginalized others. But identity can also divide us and keep us from building coalitional politics. As political scientist Cathy Cohen has argued, positioning queer identity in opposition to straight identity can keep us from seeing how heteronormativity is harming most, if not all, of us. For instance, a heterosexual mother of color who is single and raising her kids alone is also marginalized by heteronormativity, which privileges whiteness, heterosexual coupledom, and the nuclear family. If we are going to challenge and dismantle these oppressive structures, we must eschew these restrictive categories and come together around our relations to power—not our identities.[17] Identity is preventing us from getting free.

Moreover, as this book has demonstrated in previous chapters, identity can take away from pleasure, comfort, safety, respect, and countless other ways we find fulfillment in ourselves and in our relationships with others. For example, a straight or gay man may not want to explore his attraction to a trans person because it might not fit in with his definition of straight or gay identity. Or a straight man might not want to try pegging because he associates anal sex with homosexuality. Identities limit us. And the fact that we keep creating new identities—such as gynosexual, finsexual, sapiosexual, asexual, or pansexual—shows how these categories fail to capture the full complexities of gender, sexuality, and desire. Abolishing, instead of expanding, our list of sexual identities may allow us to explore all the pleasurable possibilities that life has to offer.

All of this is to say, sexual identities have got to go—heterosexuality, homosexuality, and everything else too. This idea may seem grandiose. And perhaps it is. But sexual identities are fairly new constructions of our modern society, and these identities are primarily used to control and constrain individual behavior and oppress those who refuse to conform. And yes, these identities have also served our communities in moments of collective struggle, but as this book has demonstrated, these identities ultimately function to separate us from one another and limit our possibilities for fulfillment. At this point, then, I don't know how else we can get to gender liberation and sexual freedom without abolishing them. I don't know how else we can experience the pleasures we all deserve if we continue to categorize our desires. I don't know how we can be free if compulsory heterosexuality continues to shape and structure sex, gender, and sexuality. And I don't know if trans people can find liberation if we continue to attach our identities and desires to sex, gender, and genitals. We must abolish sexual identities.

The Violence of Sexual Cissexism

In writing this book, I expect that some may view my argument about abolishing sexual identities as just a theoretical exercise. But as the interviews I've presented throughout this book have shown, sexual cissexism—how sexuality, sexual desires, sexual practices, and sexual identities maintain cisness through sexual discrimination against trans people—is a main mechanism of subordinating and marginalizing trans folks. There are material realities and consequences at stake for trans people, especially for trans people of color, including physical violence and death. Studies have shown that trans women and femmes, especially trans women and femmes of color, are at a high risk for experiencing violence, including sexual violence.[18] And homicide rates for young Black and Latina trans women and femmes are also high compared to their cis counterparts, with this victimization increasing over time.[19] Moreover, the current legislative and social backlash against trans people—which is rapidly intensifying even as I revise these pages for publication—is partly about wanting to reorient desire back toward cisness and heterosexuality, and this backlash furthers the harm that trans folks already face. I turn, then, to Faith—a 30-year-old interviewee living in Houston, Texas—to show the urgency of addressing sexual cissexism and how that process will require challenging dominant ideas of gender and sexuality, and ultimately, abolishing sexual identities.

"I was trying to leave, but I wasn't able to," said Faith, recalling a "very dangerous" date with a cishet man. "He took my phone to force me to get in his car." Afterwards, this man was "trying to get me to have sex with him, but when I didn't, he pushed me out of the car while it was going. He kind of got scared and then reversed to see if I was okay. And when I got back up, I pepper-sprayed him, and hid in somebody's yard, and called a Lyft, and waited for the Lyft to come pick me up and take me home." Having navigated Houston's dating scene for years, Faith explained how this date was "the worst date I've been on, for sure. It wasn't even a real date in the end, it was more like he kidnapped me for a couple hours, and kind of held me hostage until he kind of had enough of me throwing off his sexual advances."

Unfortunately, this violent situation wasn't unusual. "It did hurt when he pushed me out of the car," Faith recalled. "And I haven't felt upset over it since it happened because, at the same time, it's all natural in the sense that I'm used to being berated verbally, but also attacked physically." As Faith further explained, "It wasn't the first time a man has tried to attack me like that. But with a date, I think it was the first time that someone's physically attacked me." Today, Faith is "taken"—or has a boyfriend—but Faith reflected on the chronic pain that Faith still experiences from past violent encounters with previous dates. "I've been attacked before prior to that person I told you about, so that really changed a lot for me," Faith detailed. "Sometime after the attack—I did get a concussion from that attack—but sometime after, I started developing joint pain and inflammation, and it eventually got diagnosed as fibromyalgia. So, I experience chronic pain daily, and in my mind, the symptoms appeared shortly after I suffered a very serious head injury from a transphobic attack."

Violence, fear of violence, harm, vulnerability, safety—these words, as seen throughout this book, came up in many of the interviews with the trans women and femmes in this study. And while I don't want to reify the idea that trans people are just constantly navigating or experiencing violence,[20] violence and the fear of violence did shape the lives of the people in this study, including their dating and sex lives. Notably, this violence partly stems from sexual cissexism—from the sexual stereotypes of trans women and femmes. That is, the hypersexualization and dehumanization of trans women and femmes discussed in earlier chapters can and does lead to actual physical violence when navigating the dating and hookup landscape.[21] When Faith did not want to have sex with this man, he turned violent.

Moreover, these violent experiences are so prevalent as to become somewhat mundane or "natural," as Faith called it. Indeed, sexual violence, including intimate partner violence, is a main form of violence that many trans women and femmes experience and face.[22] And this violence is a main way of continuing trans subjugation. In turn, trans women and femmes often have to think about and plan to protect their safety when just trying to go on a date.[23] These experiences can also contribute to health disparities, including chronic diseases, or depression and anxiety. That is, violence and discrimination against trans people shape their health outcomes.[24] Sexual cissexism, then, harms trans people's lives. And sexual cissexism can lead to actual physical violence.

The Sexual Racism of Sexual Cissexism

These marginalizing and dehumanizing processes also intersect with race. As Faith, who is Mexican, recalled, "There have been a lot of men who have talked to me in Spanish while having sex with me. Or they call me, like, I've had men of different races call me spicy, or a tamale, or a taco, refer to my genitalia as fajitas." Faith continued, "And it comes again with either (a) not seeing us as real women, or (b) their only idea of trans women is from pornography. And it's like, they think it's acceptable in real life . . . and it's just not. A lot of us just want to be treated like human beings."

Sexual cissexism wreaks havoc and inflicts pain on trans women's and femmes' lives, especially for trans women and femmes of color. Faith links this hypersexualizing process to the fact that many people only view trans women and femmes through a pornographic lens,[25] which constructs trans women as sexual objects, not human beings. This hypersexualization, along with racial fetishization, compounds the issue for trans women and femmes of color.[26] As documented in chapter 2, sexual racism and sexual cissexism go hand-in-hand to maintain dominant desires—and related notions of masculinity and femininity—as white and cis. And as Faith's story demonstrates, these intersecting processes have real material consequences from objectification and dehumanization to chronic pain and physical violence.

In order, then, to address this harm, we must take seriously the intersection of sexual cissexism and sexual racism. To do so, we need to see and understand that cisness intersects with whiteness, and hence, cisness harms all people of color.[27] A coalitional politics can show how cisness harms not only trans people but most cis people too. For instance, Black cis women often experience gender and racial policing and discrimination for not conforming to dominant cis notions of middle-class white femininity.[28] Focusing, though, on identity can miss how cisness can also harm cis people. Challenging, then, sexual cissexism and cisness—which also means challenging sexual racism and white supremacy—must be an integral part of our work towards gender liberation for all.

The Material Harms of Sexual Identities

Faith went on to explain how ideas about sexuality and sexual identities limit us and shape these harrowing violent experiences. "There's this idea that men being affectionate and kind is gay or something, or queer, and I'm just like, it's normal," Faith stated. "Humans should be nice to each other. We should lift each other up." Ideas about sexual identities can limit how people express themselves. Furthermore, ideas about sexual identities can shape how people respond to their attraction toward trans people. As Faith explained, "The truth is, a lot of men interested in trans people—trans men, trans women, nonbinary people—don't realize that their interest stems from just being attracted to bodies. Like, it's not necessarily that they're attracted to genitals." Faith went on to give a specific example. "When I was younger, people would see me from behind, and tell other people they thought I was attractive, and then when they realized I was trans, and they're scoping me out, they acted like they weren't attracted to me," Faith detailed. "But that didn't cancel out their physical attraction to me at all, and that's kind of what ends up turning into violence is that they can't deal with that attraction."

Gender policing becomes a tool to maintain cisness and compulsory heterosexuality. People police their own gender. Some men may not want to be affectionate or kind because they associate those behaviors with women or with homosexuality. People also police other people's gender—like telling boys not to cry or hug each other. But the fact that we feel compelled to police each other shows there is nothing inherent about gender. If boys were not meant to cry, they just naturally wouldn't cry. We police gender to maintain the illusion that gender is fixed and inherent. Furthermore, policing gender helps us police sexuality and maintain similar illusions. For example, people may shame a boy for so-called "feminine" traits or behaviors out of a fear that the child might turn out to be gay.[29] Gender policing, then, is partly about orienting gender, desire, and sexuality back to both cisness and heterosexuality and about maintaining the farce that gender and sexual identities are natural, immutable, and inherent.

These processes have devastating effects. Not only do they limit us all in enjoying our full range of human feelings and experiences, but they have an undeniable connection to actual violence against trans people and anyone else who does not conform to cisness and compulsory heterosexuality. As Faith stated, some people may turn to violence to deal with their own attraction to trans people. Indeed, when people encounter trans folks, they can expand their ideas about gender and sexuality, or they may turn to violence or rejection to reinvest in these dominant notions of cisness and compulsory heterosexuality.[30] Similarly, when someone is attracted to a trans person, they can either work to further understand their own desires and sexuality or respond with violence to try and reassert their own adherence to traditional gender and sexual norms. In other words, a straight man who feels shame over his attraction to a trans woman might violently attack her to stabilize his own sense of heterosexuality. Violence becomes a disturbing and tragic way in which some people police gender and sexuality to try to maintain ahistorical myths of heterosexuality and binary gender as being natural and inherent. We cannot view, then, the oppression of trans people through just a gender-based lens. These investments in compulsory heterosexuality and sexual identities work together to explain why society seeks to harm and eliminate trans people. Trans people challenge our dominant views of sex, gender, and heterosexuality; those who are wedded to such views see trans people as a threat and respond by passing harmful laws and enacting violence against them. Fixed notions of gender and sexuality create real violence and harm, from the White House to intimate relationships.

Sexual Identities Limit Pleasure and Attraction

Faith's story also reflects how ideas about sexual identities limit pleasure. "What's funny is when I think of sex with trans people, I think of it as more intimate, more tender, more loving, obviously, more pleasurable for both sides, more mutually pleasurable," Faith explained. "Sometimes, when I think of sex with cishet men, I think of it as being transactional." For Faith, identity can be a culprit in these differing experiences of pleasure: "Now, a lot of times with trans women, these cishet men don't want to eat ass or suck some girl dick. And I don't know, they still have not gotten past it. They still associate that kind of stuff with homosexuality or something." One cis man, surprisingly, showed Faith that change is possible. "He was not afraid to do any of that," Faith recalled. "He was not afraid to kiss me, either, and again, that's something that I don't find with every hookup. So, it was the first time I felt pleasure in a way that, like, no other person was providing for me."

As previous chapters have demonstrated, sexual identities can limit sexual pleasure, comfort, and fulfillment. In turn, trans people may find more pleasure with each other. These trans for trans (t4t) relationships—as the last chapter discussed—can open up new ways of relating to others through intimacy, pleasure, love, and tenderness. t4t can move away from dominant ways of thinking about genitals, gender, cisness, and sexual identity, and thereby expose how sexual identities limit pleasure and desire. But as one of Faith's pleasurable experiences with a cis man also shows, t4t does not have to be the only solution to finding pleasure. In disassociating sex acts with ideas of sexual identity, new pleasurable possibilities can emerge for us all.

Notably, though, sexual identity categories can even affect trans people's own ideas around sexuality. "It took me a long time to realize that I was pansexual. I had been so dealing with cishet men for so many years that I didn't even realize I was attracted to other trans women, or that I was attracted to cis women," Faith explained. "But when you're younger, you kind of just go with what you know, and at first, I just thought it was homosexuality, heterosexuality, right? I thought I was just attracted to men, and I'm not attracted to women. I didn't know."

New identity terms such as *pansexual*, which has grown in popularity among Gen Z, can challenge compulsory heterosexuality and the hetero/homo binary, while also embracing attraction to a broader spectrum of gender identities. Indeed, bisexuality has long challenged this binary, with bi activists asserting their attraction to their own and other genders. Notably, trans people are more likely to identify as bi or pan compared to cis people,[31] perhaps suggesting that when someone questions their place in the gender binary, they may also question the binary notions of sexuality that it relies on. Of course, though, compulsory heterosexuality has tried to delegitimize bisexuality, pansexuality, and other nonheterosexual identities. For instance, bisexual and pansexual people are often stereotyped as confused or as just gay.[32] Nonetheless, this growing urge to expand categories of sexual identity show that sex, gender, sexuality, and desire are much more complicated than *heterosexual* and *homosexual* can capture. Even so, the hetero/homo binary remains intact through a dominant society that invalidates these other sexual identities. Expanding the list of sexual identities, then, falls short of dismantling compulsory heterosexuality, even as it gives some people, including Faith, more room to understand themselves and explore their desires and attractions. We should question, then, if an ever-expanding list of identities is an effective liberation strategy, as stigma remains prevalent for any identity that isn't heterosexual. Abolishing sexual identities altogether might be a more effective way—or perhaps the only way—to get free.

Abolition Feminism and Getting Free

Importantly, it must be noted that this idea of abolishing sexual identities is related to other abolitionist politics. Delilah—a married, white computer programmer who opened this chapter talking about transmisogyny and the obsession with tying genitals to sexual orientation—recognized the link between gender liberation and other freedom struggles. "You have to be okay with undoing a bunch of stuff about how women are supposed to be," explained Delilah. "I'm also a big fan of abolishing police and a whole bunch of consequential systemic racism shit that goes along with it that I do not experience, but you would need to fix that in order to make things safer for all the trans women." In addition to prisons and policing, Emily—who talked about t4t and gender exploration in the last chapter—also discussed issues like homelessness and poverty that many trans people face today. "There's a lot of trans people that don't have wealth," Emily explained. "Like they have no resources, they're homeless." Gender liberation, then, is tied not only to ending misogyny and transphobia but also to addressing other social issues such as prisons, police, poverty, and homelessness.

More than just an academic theory, abolition feminism is tied to gender liberation. In its modern incarnation, abolitionism is a politics of refusing to assign people to disposability.[33] Prisons, police, poverty, and homelessness are all processes and experiences of disposing of people whom society deems inferior or undeserving—of throwing them away, of relegating them to the furthest margins of society. And part of dehumanizing trans and gender-expansive people has been through constructing trans people as deviants and as criminals.[34] Crossdressing used to be illegal. Sex acts that did not lead to procreation were outlawed as "sodomy" until the early 2000s. And even today, harmful stereotypes that trans people are pedophiles and rapists are used to deny trans people access to public restrooms.[35] These processes have devastating effects, especially for trans women and femmes of color. For instance, trans women, especially trans women of color, are still often profiled by police as sex workers.[36] And close to one in two Black trans women will be incarcerated at some point in their lifetime.[37] These state-sponsored processes maintain cisness as the norm within society, while deeply harming trans people. Abolition feminism exposes, then, how the state supports and enacts gender and sexual violence against trans people, while also criminalizing them.[38]

As Delilah and growing numbers of trans people and community activists understand, individualized, identity-based politics will not save us. To get trans women free, especially trans women of color, we need a coalitional politics that also addresses systemic racism, including how policing and prisons harm trans people, especially trans people of color.[39] In other words, abolishing prisons and police is necessary for trans liberation. More broadly, global capitalist forces often lock trans people out of the formal economy. Discrimination in the workplace and housing means that trans people—especially Black and Latinx trans people—face high rates of poverty and homelessness.[40] These material realities keep trans people deeply marginalized, disposable, and on the peripheries of society. A feminist abolition politics tells us to challenge and dismantle all institutions that police gender, race, and sexuality. Addressing transmisogyny, then, requires not only abolishing sexual identities but also abolishing police and prisons and ending poverty and homelessness. We need to dismantle institutions that police and harm us all.

Following a feminist abolitionist politics, we need to build life-affirming institutions that support—not police and punish—trans people and expansive expressions of gender and sexuality.[41] A coalitional politics shows how institutions are currently harming many, if not all, of us and how we need to work together to dismantle these institutions and build new ones that affirm the value of all human life. In redesigning our institutions and society to affirm life and all its pleasures, we may also escape the prison of sexual identities that control and shape our desires.

What the Hell Happens to Gender?

Okay, so we abolish sexual identities. But then, what the hell happens to gender? Do notions of gender expand? Do we also abolish gender identities? What is gender's purpose if it is no longer tied to labeling our sexual desires? In this section, I suggest some ways gender could possibly change in a world where our sexualities, sexual identities, and desires are no longer tied to gender essentialism, the gender binary, and cisness.

Rejecting Gender Categories

Gender—like sexuality—is so much more complicated and complex than "man" or "woman" could ever fully capture. Indeed, when folks in this study were asked "What is your gender?" they often gave paragraph-length descriptions—not a simple demographic answer of man, woman, nonbinary, or something else. For instance, Chic, whose comfort story ended chapter 3, described gender as "nebulous." As Chic explained, "I kinda like rejecting the idea of gender. I'm just like an animal, kind of, you know? Like, what the fuck is gender? I'm not worried about gender. I don't hold myself to any specific standards with gender. It's shifting. It's fluid. It's fun to fuck with."

Rejecting gender categories—or at least a static understanding of gender—opens up different ways of relating to oneself and to others. But we have long known that gender is not static. Gender is contextual and interactional, and there is nothing inherent about it. An example I give in my classes is how men enact their masculinity very differently when they are at the bar or a sports game with their bros, versus when they are interacting with their mom, versus when they are on a date. If masculinity were inherent and fixed, men would always act the same, in every interaction, throughout all of history. But they don't. Because gender is shaped by our broader cultural, social, and relational contexts.[42] We need to accept that—just like those contexts—gender is fluid and ever-changing. So why do we hold tight to a gender identity if our experiences and enactments of gender constantly change? Shouldn't we just abolish gender categories?

For gender abolitionists, gender identities (like sexual identities) function as a carceral apparatus—a way to punish and control us into maintaining cisness, compulsory heterosexuality, and other dominant structures. Carceral logics are the beliefs that punishment is the best way to deal with harm and to make society safer.[43] And gender policing is a way to punish people who challenge the gender binary—with the cis assumption that the binary keeps society stable and safe. Gender abolition, then, becomes part of a larger project of refusing categorization, and thereby rejecting efforts to control, police, and punish our embodiments of gender. Instead, we can find other ways of relating to one another and building community without having to claim a gender—beyond the compulsion to claim any type of category or identity.[44] Rejecting the gender binary and abolishing gender categories can certainly help lead us toward liberation.

Decolonizing Gender

We also need to question and expose how the dominant Western ideas about gender are part of a legacy of colonialism and white supremacy. As Imani—who opened this book—explained, "I also identify [as] being nonbinary in the sense of I understand that the gender binary is a result of colonialism and the way I perceive gender is also a result of slavery and all these other things that have kind of been instilled in me." Imani continued, "So, in unpacking the fact that my view of gender is largely influenced by views that aren't of my people in Africa and in different continents. Gender isn't even really in some languages all over the world. Like, people have a third gender. People don't really even say gender." Imani's own experiences of gender are shaped and constrained by these larger historical processes and Western inventions. "I am grappling with the fact that even though I'm perceived as a trans woman, I know that I'm more of a person living and experiencing gender as a woman," explained Imani. "But that doesn't mean that I'm necessarily a woman in the Western sense of the word. That's just how I have to interpret it and how I have to present it because of the constraints of society and culture."

As discussed throughout this book, the invention of heterosexuality, sexual identities, and the gender binary are tied up not only with cisness but also with the history of white supremacy and colonialism. Historically, colonizers and enslavers used Eurocentric, Christianity-based, binary views of gender and sexuality—specifically the "man + woman = reproduction" idea of the nuclear family—as proof of modernity and civilization.[45] These colonizers partly justified their oppression, genocide, and enslavement of Indigenous and African people through constructing these communities as primitive and deviant for having "third" genders and expansive expressions of gender and sexuality.[46] Colonial forces also enacted violence against gender-expansive people, especially trans-feminized people, to justify stealing land for imperialist expansion.[47] For example, Spanish colonizers would feed the *joyas*—a third gender among Indigenous people in what became

California—to their mastiffs. To tolerate, harbor, or associate with a third-gender person meant death.[48] The gender binary itself is a colonial imposition, and the categories of "man" and "woman" are settler colonial creations.[49] In addition to enforcing the gender binary, settler colonialism also worked to reinforce the heterosexual nuclear family as the norm over expansive definitions of families; colonizers saw transgressive sexualities and extended family formations as savagery that justified their violence and conquering.[50] Heterosexuality, sexual identities, and the Eurocentric gender binary are patriarchal, white supremacist, settler colonial imperial projects.

Imani's comments also point to how many precolonial cultures did not even have a language of gender. In *The Invention of Women*, sociologist Oyèrónkẹ́ Oyěwùmí shows how in Yoruba culture, for example, there was no language for gender before colonialism.[51] Yoruba society was organized around age and other ways of relating, not around supposed biological differences between sexed and gendered bodies.[52] Contrary to popular assumptions, sex and gender binaries are not some universal truths that have existed throughout time or even throughout all societies and cultures. Many cultures had multiple genders or no gender. But through colonialism, imperialism, and slavery, Europeans enforced the gender binary and heterosexuality on Indigenous people. Imani recognized the constraints of these Western categories. And in this recognition and Imani's own understanding of womanhood, there is an opening to change these categories and ways of relating.

Other interviewees also saw expanding gender and experiencing gender beyond the binary as ways to push back against oppressive Eurocentric ideas. For instance, Emma, who in chapter 3 discussed how the word *gay* could delegitimize trans women's womanhood, also talked about the limits of language in capturing experiences of gender: "I would say in a way to describe my gender specifically, I don't necessarily see it as, on a scale of male to feminine, I'd say of course feminine. The way I word it to my friends is 'I am woman according to your language and your people.'" For Emma, gender is an expression of self, like art. "I feel as though my gender can be more so accurately depicted and defined through music, and dance, and art," Emma explained. "So, I learned at camp this term called xenogender. Xenogender is essentially perceiving gender through sensory and through things that commonly wouldn't be associated with gender." Emma gave an example. "Because before when I was first starting to come into my identity I was like, 'I don't know what my gender is. My gender is dance. My gender is art.' I was mentioning my gender is the ocean," Emma stated. "So, all of these non-gender-related things are my gender."

Xenogender goes beyond our current human understandings of gender, or at least, beyond the Eurocentric gender binary. In doing so, xenogender troubles cis understandings of gender and expands gender beyond the binary. And while the term xenogender might be new, these experiences of gender are not. Indigenous practices have often related gender to the spirit—beyond the human body.[53] And gender expansiveness rooted in Indigeneity can be a main method of challenging Eurocentric ways of thinking about and performing gender.[54] This approach shows that how we understand sex and gender today in the West is in and through colonial logics and colonialism.[55] And hence, Indigenous understandings can challenge the gender binary as a universal truth and can help us achieve gender liberation.[56] Decolonizing gender represents an essential approach in getting us to freedom.

Enjoying and Exploring Gender

For 22-year-old Juanita, exploring joy and euphoria can be the foundation of exploring gender. "I was talking to someone—I think we ended up going on a few dates—who was on the fence about their gender identity," explained Juanita, a Tejana living in Boston, Massachusetts, while working as an assistant project manager for a Cherokee language archive. "And so, I started talking about—and this is something I talk about with a lot of my friends as well—is trans joy as a form of liberation over trans suffering, which is often how media portrays transgender care, whether it's in support or against us, it's often through the lens of suffering." Juanita continued, "We had a long conversation on a date about using trans joy and euphoria as a way to explore identity as opposed to dysphoria and how maybe you feel okay with your body, but if there's something that makes you feel even better about it, it's worth exploring that and listening to that."

Juanita, who was partnered (but available) during the time of the study, points to how discussions of trans people are often about trans suffering, a lens that often constructs trans people as "vulnerable subjects."[57] To challenge this framework and to make visible other aspects of trans lives, one can focus on joy, care, and euphoria.[58] For Juanita, joy can be a form of liberation. Part of this liberation is how joy can trouble static, binary notions of gender. If something feels good, it might be worth exploring, even if it goes against dominant understandings of gender. Certain forms of pleasure and joy—especially those that challenge limited ideas of gender, identity, and embodiment—can guide us to alternative ways of building relationships with one another, with ourselves, and in building a more liberated world.

We might, then, not abolish gender entirely. But we may abolish the gender binary, static notions of gender, and maybe even gender identities. Indeed, so many trans women and femmes in this study gave lengthy answers in describing their own gender. And in a 2022 population survey of trans adults, six in ten did not identify as a man or woman but described themselves with more expansive terminology such as *nonbinary* or *gender-nonconforming*. Around half also used they/them pronouns.[59] Many trans people already have more expansive views of gender simply because of their life experiences. Nevertheless, as dominant notions of gender are intertwined with compulsory heterosexuality,[60] gender will change when we abolish sexual identities. Challenging the Eurocentric gender binary, abolishing the carceral apparatus of gender, decolonizing gender, and using joy and pleasure to explore gender can all be strategies to rethink gender outside of identities and the binary. Through these processes, we may all be freer to express ourselves however we desire.

The Pleasure of Becoming and Relating

While on a walk one evening, a nonacademic friend and I talked about identity. I go on walks with this friend about once a week, a practice we began during the pandemic, and have continued, despite moving to different neighborhoods. If I must list her identities, she is a Lebanese, straight, cis woman who owns her own graphic design company. We don't share a singular identity in common, except we are both from Ohio (but who wants to claim an Ohio identity?). Nonetheless, we deeply relate to one another and enjoy each other's company. So, what is the point of identity? Can't we build relationships—including deeply meaningful and loving ones—outside of shared identities? And can our insistence on identifying and categorizing ourselves be thwarting us from building more meaningful relationships and communities? My friend and I think so.

Indeed, sexual identities make sexuality a property—some individualistic way of owning one's desires. Sexual identities, then, take away from how sexuality should be a mode of relating, *not* a possession.[61] And as this book has shown, sexual identities structure our desires in and through cisness, often by upholding gender essentialism. In turn, sexual identities harm trans people. But what if we saw sexuality as a mode of relating to others and expressing our desires through comfort, care, pleasure, consent, safety, respect, trust, and communication—and not as something we possess or that defines who we are? We literally don't need sexual labels. And these sexual labels are thwarting pleasure, precluding our ability to experience the complexities and range of our desires, and not letting us fully relate to other humans in ways that are possible, positive, and life-affirming. We should see, then, sexuality as sets of relations—as ways to exchange and reciprocate with each other—not as categories or objects. That is, we must resist objectifying the intersubjective, whereby identity essentially turns our relationships into objects.[62] Identity is often an individualistic idea—some unchanging thing we hold as essential to our being.[63] But we are not static, unchanging people. We are always in relation, always becoming.[64]

Comfort can be a way to think about relating and becoming. Indeed, a lot has been written about trans joy and trans care. But care, connection, communication, joy, pleasure, and other things we often associate with a good life and good relationships are often shaped and informed by comfort. Comfort can be foundational for experiencing joy, euphoria, and pleasure. And if pleasure is a measure of freedom,[65] then comfort might be a mode of relating that gets us closer to that freedom. Comfort itself might also be a measure of freedom and a mode of relating that moves us beyond identities to actually connecting and caring for each other as humans. Comfort can point us to another world—a better world—where we can live without fear and worry. It centers care and communication in experiencing good sex, great dates, and orgasmic pleasure. It provides us with world-building strategies to work toward a better tomorrow.

t4t can also show us the complexities of relating. t4t relationships are a strategy against cisness to find safety; but as an identity strategy, t4t is fraught. Gender identity—including trans identity—is complicated by race, class, and other social categories and experiences. And trans people can harm other trans people. t4t is not always or inherently safe. But components of t4t, such as care, safety, and connection, can teach us important modes of relating, which can be crucial to building relationships and communities with others, including building coalitional politics that don't privilege identity. t4t also shows how centering trans pleasure can challenge the pleasure deficit that many trans people may face. By challenging cis ideas of gender and pleasure, t4t paves new paths toward liberation and freedom that affirm trans lives and that help us reimagine ourselves in relation to the world.

So, let us imagine relating and becoming beyond sexual identities. Imagine not having to "come out" because there are no sexual identities to claim, and no sexual identity is privileged over any others. We don't use sexual identity to relate to one another—no pathologizing racist ideas of sexuality such as being on the "down low,"[66] no bisexuality or gay identity to "hide" as these categories do not exist, have no meaning, and do not privilege heterosexuality. In this imaginary world, we are all free to explore our desires with any and all people, consensually and justly. I mean, truly: Imagine a world without compulsory heterosexuality. Women do not have to build their lives around finding a man to marry, nor are they subjugated by the various ways gender inequality unfolds within heterosexual relationships.[67] Men too are not limited to the acceptable "masculine" emotional expressions of anger and violence; boys and men get to cry, without shame, when they're sad. We can all be free to explore our pleasures and find new ways of relating and becoming in and through comfort, care, pleasure, consent, respect, trust, and love.

After the imagining comes the practice. If you've read this far, perhaps you feel ready to begin questioning your desires and your identities. Where did they come from? Why are they meaningful to you? What could your life look like if you didn't label your desires? How can you relate to others if identity is not a basis for connection? Perhaps, today, you lean into some pleasure and joy and see where it takes you. Pleasure can be a politic to help us reach a new horizon of gender liberation. So, try that new sex toy. Reach out to the person or persons you find attractive and see if they are also interested. Try on that outfit you've been eyeing. Find a new erogenous zone. Explore your body in a mirror. Try a new name or pronoun for yourself. Just explore, and let your desires and pleasures guide the way. Another world is possible. But identities are part of what is stopping us from getting there. Let us lean, then, into the pleasure of relating and becoming. Let us center comfort, care, pleasure, consent, respect, trust, and love as modes of relating that get us to a better tomorrow. And let us continue the work of getting us *all* free.

Pleasure. That sensual gratification. A sometimes-tactile sensation. Tingling. A tingling that one may very well feel in their groin. But also, a yearning for freedom. For liberation. Euphoria. Praise. Joy. Affirmation. The feeling of a lover or lovers kissing your neck. The pleasure of leaving your home without fear of harassment and discrimination. The pleasure of having a partner or partners inside of your body. The pleasure of community, of friendship, of connection. The pleasure of that toe-curling orgasm. The pleasure of embodying your innermost desires. The pleasure of receiving a compliment. The pleasure of being yourself. The pleasure of a kink, a fetish. The pleasure of expressing the multiple and voluminous ways gender resides in and through the body. The pleasure of transforming the body. The pleasure of feeling comfortable, of feeling safe. The pleasure of being desired. The pleasure of not having to label our desires for someone else's understanding. The pleasure of recognition. The pleasure of knowing that our pleasures are connected to others. The pleasure of another life, a better life. The pleasure of gender liberation. The pleasure of becoming. The possibilities of pleasure.

METHODOLOGICAL APPENDIX A

t4t as Methods

I offer this methodological appendix as a trans for trans (t4t) strategy—of building an intellectual community around trans knowledge production. My goal for this appendix is to aid other scholars in learning more about doing this type of research. I provide this appendix, then, to help other trans studies scholars who are applying for Institutional Review Board approval or for grants, or who are trying to justify their project to their advisor, or who just want to learn from trans people and from studying sex and sexuality. This appendix is my way to try to support other trans studies scholars and to show how we can care for each other and our participants while doing trans methods and while creating trans knowledge production that decenters cisness within academia. More specifically, as a t4t strategy, this appendix offers other trans studies scholars ways we can center trans voices and trans pleasure in our work. It also presents some ethical practices on how we can care for the trans people whom we are asking to be in our studies. We need to affirm and validate trans people, including the trans people who agree to participate in research. Centering aspects of t4t— such as care, community, safety, and consent—can be a methodological approach to doing ethical trans research studies.

Reddit and Studying Online Spaces

The concept of t4t began online—on Craigslist.org. The internet, then, is (and has been) a place for trans folks to find one another, support one another, and learn about and from other trans people.[1] As trans participants in this study discussed, trans people such as Imani (who opened this book) learned through social media that one does not have to be heterosexual or feminine in order to be a trans woman. And as seen in chapter 2, trans people also pushed back at the discriminatory online discourses about trans people. A t4t methodology that is committed to affirming and validating trans people needs to take seriously online spaces, as these spaces can provide a unique platform for studying discourses about trans people, about trans resistance, about trans folks providing community and care for one another, and about how our own thinking about gender and sexuality can expand.

Indeed, online forums enable interaction between people who might not ever interact offline.[2] The internet has also become a tool for both cis and trans people to learn about trans-related issues and policies that they can apply to offline interactions.[3] Moreover, seeing cis people and trans people interact—especially seeing trans people pushing back at cis people's logics and posts—provides a level of interactional analysis that challenges cisness and that would be hard to study in most offline places. In line with the tenet of t4t safety, there could also be a level of protection online—even despite all the transphobia online—where trans people can feel more comfortable to resist and to push back at logics that uphold cisness. Online spaces are rich sites, then, in studying discourses about the social world, including discourses about gender, sexuality, and trans folks. Online spaces are also rich sites in studying challenges to cisness and heterosexuality. We need to continue to study them more.

I offer up how I studied an internet space in hopes of helping others to continue studying these various online realms. For this study, I analyzed a large sample of Reddit discussion posts, threads, and "subreddits." Reddit is an online community or "a community of communities"[4] comprised of forums, discussion posts and threads, "subreddits" devoted to specific community posts and topics, and a social news aggregation website.[5] As of September 2021, according to Statista—a market and consumer data company—Reddit was the nineteenth most visited site in the world and the seventh most visited site in the United States. A study by Pew Research found that YouTube and Reddit were the only two online social media platforms that saw statistically significant growth since 2019, with Reddit being the tenth most used online platform as reported by U.S. adults.[6] As a popular site, Reddit is an apt place to study how people discursively construct and talk about gender, sexuality, and desires.

I examined Reddit posts from April 2021 to June 2021. I used search terms such as "transgender," "dating transgender," "sex transgender," and "transamorous" to find posts. I also explored subreddits such as r/asktransgender, r/transpersonals, r/t4m, r/m4t, r/chasersrisseup, and r/transamorous. And I also found discussions across a variety of other subreddits, including on LGBTQIA+ subreddits such as r/lgbt and r/transeducate, on the subreddit r/FeMRADebates that discusses feminism and men's rights activism, and on numerous general subreddits such as r/NoStupidQuestions, r/Discussion, and r/AskReddit. I often clicked on posts and threads related to the thread I was reading and explored Reddit in a way that users would. Through this process, I created a data set of over two hundred downloaded posts and their threads. This sample of posts and threads were the entirety of posts and threads that I could find during the three-month period of data collection that were either on the subreddits or were posts I discovered from my search terms. Many posts were recent (i.e., within the past year). But some posts and threads were started over five years ago. Some posts in my sample had no comments. Others had around twenty comments. A smaller group had hundreds of comments, and one post had over ten thousand comments. I do not anonymize the usernames as the posts are public and the usernames are another form of data and mean-making.

I began with close readings of the selected posts and threads to become familiar with the patterns of how users talked and engaged.[7] From there, I analyzed all downloaded posts and threads in MAXQDA. Following a grounded theory analytical approach, I engaged in close readings of selected posts and threads and did a line-by-line coding of these posts and threads to get an analytical grasp on how people were discussing trans people, gender, sexuality, and desire.[8] I then moved to flexible coding, whereby I used the analytical insights from the initial coding to code larger swaths of posts and threads.[9] Through this iterative process, I generated over one hundred codes (e.g., chaser, femininity, masculinity, misogyny, submission). Notably, while online comments might be performative and who people say they are online might not be who they are offline, all identities are performative, and studying online forums can document one way that people manage, negotiate, and reformulate their identities and desires.[10] The analysis, then, is not trying to reveal some "truth" about gender and sexuality, but rather, to see how people discursively construct their sense of gender and sexuality in relation to trans women and femmes.[11]

Moving forward, I hope that trans studies scholars continue to study online spaces. We need to continue to understand how online spaces are opening up ideas about gender and sexuality while simultaneously upholding cisness. We also need to know how trans folks are using online spaces to meet each other and support each other. And we need to further grasp how trans people use online spaces to resist and to find pleasure. Additionally, we need to know how online spaces can provide community, care, and safety in ways the offline world may not afford trans folks. There is much to learn about online spaces in relation to gender, sexuality, and trans people. We need to continue that work.

t4t Ethics of Interviewing

Most of this book is based on qualitative interviews with 48 trans women and femmes in the United States. All interviews were conducted from September 2022 to November 2022. The broader interview study and guide sought to understand the dating, hookup, and sex lives of trans women and femmes. Interviews were structured to last an hour, though many interviews went longer. Methodological Appendix B provides the interview guide.

Notably, a t4t ethics that centers care, community, and affirming trans lives shaped how these interviews were conducted. For this study, this ethics included several aspects: paying trans people, focusing on pleasure in trans people's lives, and letting trans voices help guide the interview process. These t4t aspects of the research process validated trans experiences and helped to build rapport with the trans people in this study.

Regarding a t4t ethics around compensation, each person received $100 for participating. They could get the money either through Paypal or as a Visa gift card. (Almost everyone chose Paypal.) As trans women are a hard-to-reach population, it is standard procedure to compensate well for their time in order to increase response rates of this highly stigmatized group.[12] Moreover, offering no or little compensation can lead to only people from higher socioeconomic groups being more likely to participate.[13] I selected, then, the amount of $100 as that amount felt ethical in asking a vulnerable population to participate in research with me. We need to recognize the material realities of trans people, and we need to compensate them for their time. Of course, I must also acknowledge that I work at an R1 university with resources that make it easier to provide compensation to research participants. But if we don't pay people, we may not be able to capture a diverse group of trans voices, especially the voices of more precarious trans folks.

The 48 trans women and femmes were recruited through a recruitment flyer. The flyer asked, "Are you a trans woman, trans femme, and/or trans feminine person who wants to talk about your dating and sex life?" The eligibility requirements to be recruited were: be a trans woman and/or trans femme, be 18 years of age or older, live in the United States, and be able to speak English. The flyer also explained that it would be a one-hour interview on Zoom and that participants would receive $100 at the end of the interview. I posted the recruitment flyer on my own Twitter account. (And yes, it was still called Twitter back then.) I also sent the recruitment flyer to some friends and colleagues to share with their own networks, and I sent the recruitment flyer to some trans organizations. On the flyer, participants were directed to a link to fill out an eligibility form. The screening questions on this form asked: "Do you identify as transgender, nonbinary, and/or as a gender different than the one assigned at birth?"; "Please describe for me your gender identity"; "Please describe for me your sexual identity"; "Please describe for me your race or racial identity"; "How old are you?"; "Do you live in the United States?"; "Is there anything else you would like to share or that you would like me to know about you participating in this study?"

Within twelve hours of posting the recruitment flyer, over one hundred people filled out the screening survey. As I did not have over $10,000 dollars to pay over one hundred people to participate in the study, I had to quickly shut down the recruitment portion of the study. I then selected people to contact to be interviewed for the study. I tried to select a diverse group of people based on race, age, and location. Later, while people were being interviewed, I was informed by participants in the study that the flyer had gone viral. People found the recruitment flyer on dating apps and on other social media outlets that I didn't post on. There was a type of t4t solidarity of wanting to share this flyer with other trans folks and across various trans networks.

I partly think, though, that the viral nature of the recruitment flyer and the ease of recruiting people into this study came from offering $100 for a one-hour interview. When we pay people for their time, they are probably more likely to want to participate. And as noted, paying people allowed me to recruit a diverse range of trans women and femmes into the study. Of the 48 trans women and femmes in this study, 21 identified as non-Hispanic white and 27 identified as women and femmes of color. They ranged in age from 19 to 52 years old. The majority of the trans women and femmes were in their twenties or thirties. And the average age of the participants was 31 years old. The participants came from all over the United States such as from Tennessee and the Carolinas to California. Forty-five of the 48 identified as not straight or not heterosexual. As is common in qualitative research, all names in this book are pseudonyms to maintain confidentiality. I describe the participants in this book based on their own descriptors and identities. I also did not ask the participants their pronouns; hence, I do not use any pronouns throughout the book when talking about the participants in this study.

Aside from compensation, I also think the recruitment flyer went viral because trans women and femmes wanted to talk about their dating and sex lives. This point gets at another aspect of a t4t ethics: Trans people want to talk about pleasure and other positive aspects of their lives. Indeed, many people in the study thanked me for doing this project as they said there isn't much sex and dating research on trans people (especially outside of medical and health research). Many trans people do want to talk about the joyful, euphoric, and pleasurable moments of their lives, and many trans people in this study said that they have never been asked questions about these topics before. There seemed to be a type of t4t reciprocity of folks being genuinely interested in wanting to give their time to help a study that focused on dating, sex, and pleasure.

Once people were recruited, all interviews were conducted over Zoom by a person on the research team. Zoom was the best platform for this study, as Zoom allowed the research team to reach a broader demographic, including reaching people outside of Southern California. Indeed, Zoom interviews can extend recruitment reach and inclusivity, as they are more accessible and have no travel requirements.[14] Before the interview, each participant received a consent form. They were also informed that they could skip any questions in the interview. Each participant then gave verbal consent to participate at the start of the interview. One graduate student (Kori Pacyniak) and three undergraduate students (Shell Morales, Laura Rodriguez Pinto, Stephanie Gutierrez) conducted all the interviews. Every member on the research team was paid for being a research assistant or received course credit for their labor. Notably, I had already trained the undergraduate students in qualitative interviewing for my other research project (the Family, Housing, and Me Project), and I was confident in their fabulous and rigorous research skills based on having already worked with them.

Importantly, as part of the interview process (and as seen on the interview guide), we asked folks at the end of the interview if there was anything we didn't discuss that they thought was important. This question allowed trans people in the study to help guide the research process and to center their voices in learning what is important in relation to trans women and femmes, sex, and dating. For instance, early on in the study, many participants mentioned that they were surprised that there were no specific questions about t4t. I quickly realized that t4t was a crucial aspect of many trans people's lives, and so I told the research team to explore this topic more in their other interviews. I also focused on t4t in the analysis of the interviews.

After conducting the interviews, the qualitative interview data were professionally transcribed through a transcription service. Transcripts were entered into MAXQDA, and I coded all interviews myself. Following a grounded theory analytical approach, I conducted line-by-line coding of the first several interviews to get an analytical grasp on how people were discussing dating, sex, and hooking up.[15] I then moved to flexible coding.[16] Through this iterative process, I generated over one hundred codes (e.g., bodies, communication, connection, desire/desirability, fear, fetish, healing, joy, pleasure, resistance, safety, strategies, t4t, violence). From applying the codes to all 48 interviews, I generated 10,875 coded segments. This book is truly only the tip of the iceberg of everything that I learned. I tried, though, to capture the most salient topics that came up across the interviews.

All in all, aspects of t4t—care, consent, solidarity, reciprocity—shaped the research process. For interview-based studies, this t4t ethics can include paying people, centering positive aspects of trans lives such as pleasure, and allowing trans voices to guide both the interview process and analysis. If we use tenets of t4t such as care and consent in conducting research, we can do research studies that are ethical and that center trans lives and trans voices.

The Pleasure of Trans Knowledge Production

Research can be pleasurable. And while research is my job—and maybe we should be wary of finding pleasure in work as it might be a way to further our exploitation—I do really enjoy aspects of it. I mean, I get to think about, talk to, teach about, and study trans folks. I get to be in community with people who care about making the world a better place. And in this particular political moment of rising antitrans legislation, I find this work to be ever more important. I also think that we need to find pleasure in this work in order to sustain us in doing the work. Luckily, I found so much pleasure throughout this entire research process. Getting to design an interview guide and write questions about sex and pleasure was exciting. There isn't much academic work about trans pleasure, so I was exhilarated just thinking about what I was going to learn from the interview questions I was writing. I remember the joy I had when starting this project and how I hoped it would open up new ways of understanding trans people and their lives. The unknown of the beginning of a research project can be truly invigorating as so many different possibilities lie ahead.

And then there was the pleasure of recruitment itself. I was in awe seeing how quickly and passionately folks wanted to be in the study. Every recruitment survey that hit my inbox made me giddy. Trans women and femmes really did want to talk about their sex and dating lives. I felt like I was doing something right in designing a research study around sex, relationships, and pleasure. I felt like I was on the right path in contributing to trans studies and in having something new to say.

I also experienced so much pleasure seeing the excitement of my research team during the interview process. Each time the team met to check in about how the interviews were going and what each person was learning, the students seemed so happy to be conducting this study with me. The students were finding passion in doing qualitative research, and I found pleasure in helping to mentor them through something I fervently love—conducting research projects. Moreover, some of the participants seemed to find pleasure in talking about their dating and sex lives. Many participants said that they appreciated reflecting on these positive aspects of their lives and were thankful that there was a study documenting these pleasurable parts of trans people's lived experiences. There was a pleasure in this reciprocity.

Of course, I also found pleasure in writing about pleasure. It was truly inspiring to write about how trans women and femmes are making lives for themselves and challenging dominant social structures. It was compelling to write about how the pleasure of freedom and liberation can get us to a better tomorrow. And it was fun to think through new ideas such as comfort as a mode of relation that can help us work toward this new future. I love writing. And getting to write about these understudied, yet important, topics made writing all the more pleasurable. I would also be remiss to not mention that I also found so much pleasure and community workshopping each chapter of this book with my writing group. Their feedback on this book truly illuminated what the positive aspects of t4t look like—their care, community, and solidarity touched every page of this book. I am thankful every day for my writing group, and I was always animated to revise the book again after getting their brilliant feedback. The pleasure of a great writing group can be life-giving.

Moving forward, as pleasure is a measure of freedom,[17] centering a pleasure politic in our work can be crucial in liberating methods and knowledge production from cisnormative and other dominant ways of doing research. The pleasure of being trans, the pleasure of doing trans studies, the pleasure of conducting research—the multiplicities of pleasure can work to continue to disrupt dominant ways of producing knowledge while also nourishing us in doing this work.[18] Importantly, and as I hope this book has demonstrated, trans knowledge production should value and center pleasure, as this pleasure sustains trans people to continue to exist despite a world that tries to eliminate trans people. We need to center trans pleasure in order to produce knowledge that disrupts normative ways of knowing, and hence, gives us a better understanding of our social world and how to get to an actual better tomorrow.

My hope is that this book and methodological appendix help in paving a path forward in finding pleasure within knowledge production. I offer, then, this entire book as a t4t strategy—of being in and building community with other trans scholars and scholars who want us all to get free. Like any t4t strategy, this book is probably not perfect. And other folks, including other trans folks, will probably disagree with some of the arguments. But let us continue the conversation and let us do the work of getting to sexual freedom and gender liberation. Let us find pleasure in being in community, including being in intellectual community, with one another. And let us center pleasure and new ways of doing research and producing knowledge in order to think and relate differently. Thank you for going on this journey. May we continue down this path of loving and caring for one another. And may we all be free someday.

METHODOLOGICAL APPENDIX B

Interview Guide

Opening Questions
1. In your own words, can you describe for me what the term *gender* means to you?
2. In your own words, can you describe for me what the term *transgender* means to you?
3. Can you tell me what you enjoy about being trans?

Dating
1. When people talk about dating, what comes to mind?
2. Could you tell me about where you typically look for people to go on dates with?
   a. Could you walk me through the steps from beginning to end on how you go about this process?
3. Can you tell me about the most recent date you've been on?
   a. What was memorable about it?
4. How does this date compare to other dates you've been on / people you've dated?
5. Can you think of a date that went really well and describe it for me?
6. Can you think of a date that was a disaster and describe it for me?
7. Can you tell me about the type of people you normally date?
8. What are some things that you consider when deciding whether to date someone?

a. Why are these things important to you?
   b. Can you specifically describe for me a time when you used these traits to decide about going or not going on a date?
9. Have you ever found it difficult to try to date/contact certain types of people?
   a. How so?
10. Could you describe for me how you navigate discussing being trans before or while on a date?
    a. Do you recall a conversation during a date where you being trans came up?
        i. Would you please share with me?
11. Could you tell me about some worries you have when it comes to dating and going on dates?
    a. What do you see as the main challenges in your dating life?
12. Could you tell me about some things that you enjoy or that bring you pleasure when it comes to dating and going on dates?
13. If you could design a dating app that centers trans women, what would it look like?

Representation

1. When you think about the depiction of trans people's dating and sex experiences within popular media, what comes to mind?
   a. What is your reaction to this representation?
2. How do you think depictions of trans women in popular media (e.g., TV, movies, social media) have shaped how people you date might perceive you?
3. Could you describe for me your own experiences watching trans people on TV and in movies and how it has shaped your own understanding of being trans and your sexuality?
4. How do you think TV shows, movies, and social media are opening up trans representation around dating and sex?

Sex

1. When people talk about hooking up, what comes to mind?
2. When people talk about sex, what comes to mind?

3. Could you describe for me how you view sex and hooking up similarly?
   a. Differently?
4. Could you tell me where you typically look for people to hook up with?
5. Can you tell me about the most recent hookup you've had?
6. How does this hookup compare to other hookups you've had?
7. Can you think of a hookup that went really well and describe it for me?
8. Can you think of a hookup that was a disaster and describe it for me?
9. Could you describe for me how you navigate discussing being trans before engaging in sex with someone?
10. What types of people do you find are most often attracted to you?
11. Could you describe for me a moment when you felt you were fetishized or objectified during a sexual interaction?
    a. How did it feel?
12. Could you describe for me what it feels like to be desired or to have someone desire you?
13. Could you tell me about some worries you have when it comes to hooking up and having sex?
14. Could you tell me about some things that you enjoy or that bring you pleasure when it comes to hooking up and having sex?
    a. Can you describe for me a specific time when you experienced this pleasure?

Demographic Questions

1. How would you describe your gender identity?
2. How would you describe your sexual identity?
3. What is your current relationship status?
4. Your age?
5. And what type of work do you do? That is, what is your current role at your job?
6. Educational background?
7. Race?
8. What city do you currently live in?

Closing Questions

1. What do you think needs to change to make dating and hooking up better for trans women?
2. Is there a question I did not ask that you consider would have been interesting or important for me to ask?
3. Is there something we did not discuss about trans people, dating, and sex that in your opinion would be important in helping other people understand what it's like to be in your shoes?
4. What advice would you give to a trans person who has just started dating?
5. What advice would you give to your younger self when you had just started dating?
6. What advice would you give to a trans person who has just started navigating sex and hookups?
7. What advice would you give to your younger self when you had just started navigating sex and hookups?
8. Anything else you would like to say or add?

Notes

1. Compulsory Heterosexuality and the Trans Femme Existence

1. *Trans femme* is often used to describe trans people who identify with a feminine gender expression. Trans femme folks may identify with femininity, but they may not necessarily identify as women.
2. Rich (1980).
3. Cishet describes someone who is both cisgender (someone who identifies with the gender they were assigned at birth) and heterosexual.
4. Galupo, Mitchell, and Davis (2015).
5. Galupo, Henise, and Mercer (2016); Galupo, Mitchell, and Davis (2015); Kirzinger et al. (2023); Reisner et al. (2023).
6. Stearns (1995).
7. Butler (1990); Rich (1980).
8. Meyerowitz (2002).
9. Puckett et al. (2021).
10. Koch-Rein, Haschemi Yekani, and Verlinden (2020).
11. Billard and Zhang (2022).
12. Rich (1980).
13. Rich (1980); Ward (2020).
14. Ward (2020).
15. Rich (1980).
16. Rich (1980, 650).
17. zamantakis (2023, 3).
18. Butler (1990); Ward (2020).

19. Schilt and Lagos (2017).
20. Blair and Hoskin (2019).
21. Buggs (2020).
22. Westbrook (2020).
23. Butler (1990); Jagose (1996).
24. Vidal-Ortiz (2002).
25. zamantakis (2023).
26. Robinson (2023).
27. Collins (1990).
28. Truth (1851). We cannot know for certain what Truth exactly said in her speech. Indeed, even the title of "Ain't I a Woman?" or "Ar'n't I a Woman?" is debated. Painter (1996, 164–78).
29. Collins (2004).
30. White (1985).
31. Spillers (1987).
32. Collins (2004).
33. Ussher et al. (2022).
34. Ward (2020).
35. Johns et al. (2012).
36. Robinson (2015).
37. Meyerowitz (2002).
38. Malatino (2020); Malatino (2022).
39. Billard (2019).
40. brown (2019).

2. Sexual Cissexism

1. Chamberland (2016); Espineira (2016).
2. Espineira (2016); Robinson (2023).
3. Robinson (2023).
4. Blair and Hoskin (2019).
5. Stember (1978).
6. Holland (2012); Vidal-Ortiz, Robinson, and Khan (2018).
7. Han (2021).
8. Han (2021); Robinson (2015).
9. Han (2021).

10. Collins (2004); Davis (1981).
11. Kil (2012).
12. Vidal-Ortiz et al. (2018).
13. Serano (2007).
14. Blair and Hoskin (2019).
15. Chamberland (2016); Operario et al. (2008); Robinson (2023).
16. Sumerau, Cragun, and Mathers (2016); Sumerau and Mathers (2019).
17. Tompkins (2014).
18. Hood (2020); Tompkins (2014).
19. Hood (2020).
20. For more examples and posts, see Robinson (2023).
21. zamantakis (2023).
22. Gercio (2015).
23. Billard (2019).
24. Buggs (2020); Smilges (2020); Strings (2019).
25. Cheney (2011).
26. Cottom (2019).
27. Buggs (2020); Collins (2004); Smilges (2020).
28. DuBois and Shattuck-Heidorn (2021).
29. Burns, Beischel, and Van Anders (2024).
30. Burns et al. (2024).
31. Prunas (2019).
32. Chadwick and van Anders (2017).
33. Robinson (2023); Serano (2007).
34. Ward (2020).
35. Chamberland (2016).
36. Blair and Hoskin (2019).
37. Zamantakis (2020).
38. Kai and Devor (2022).
39. Steinbugler (2012).
40. Krell (2017).
41. Cheney (2011); Enke (2012).
42. Costello (2021).
43. Ward (2021, 113).
44. Morgensen (2010); Patil (2018); Patil (2022).
45. Ward (2021).

46. Somerville (2000).
47. Ferguson (2003); Somerville (2000).
48. Vidal-Ortiz et al. (2018).
49. For more examples and posts, see Robinson (2024).
50. Bonilla-Silva (2003).
51. Velocci (2024).
52. Serano (2024).
53. McLaughlin et al. (2023).
54. Jarne and Auld (2006); McLaughlin et al. (2023).
55. Velocci (2024).
56. Ashley (2024).
57. Henderson (2020); Patil (2018); Patil (2022).
58. Henderson (2020); Patil (2022).
59. Adjepong (2020).
60. Blank (2012); Katz (1995); Ward (2021).
61. Schilt and Westbrook (2009); Westbrook and Schilt (2014).
62. Stearns (1995).
63. Goffman (1963).
64. Ward (2012).
65. Walters (2014).
66. Schilt (2015).
67. Walters (2014).
68. Stearns (1995).
69. Broussard and Warner (2019).
70. Robinson (2015).
71. Han (2021); Robinson (2015).
72. Forbes and Stacey (2022); Robinson (2015).
73. brown (2019).

3. Comfort and the Paradox of Pleasure

1. "Comfort," accessed February 25, 2025, www.encyclopedia.com/literature-and-arts/language-linguistics-and-literary-terms/english-vocabulary-d/comfort.

2. "Comfortable," accessed February 25, 2025, www.encyclopedia.com/humanities/dictionaries-thesauruses-pictures-and-press-releases/comfortable.

3. All are direct quotes pulled from the interview transcripts of this study.
4. "Comfort," accessed February 19, 2025, https://dictionary.cambridge.org/us/dictionary/english/comfort.
5. Jones (2019); Orne (2017).
6. Jones (2019); Robinson (2022).
7. brown (2019); Robinson (2022).
8. brown (2019).
9. Austin, Papciak, and Lovins (2022); Beischel, Gauvin, and Van Anders (2022).
10. Shuster and Westbrook (2022); Westbrook (2020).
11. Rosenberg, Tilley, and Morgan (2019).
12. Davy and Toze (2018); Kai and Devor (2022).
13. Prunas (2019).
14. Kai and Devor (2022).
15. Gilbert (2020).
16. Edelman and Zimman (2014).
17. Kai and Devor (2022).
18. Albury et al. (2021); Griffiths and Armstrong (2023).
19. Muro and Martinez (2016); Ussher et al. (2022).
20. Carlström, Ek, and Gabrielsson (2021).
21. Anzani et al. (2021); Ussher et al. (2022).
22. Ussher et al. (2022).
23. Kai and Devor (2022).
24. Johns et al. (2012).
25. Robinson (2015).
26. Turley, Monro, and King (2017).
27. Robinson (2023).
28. Burns, Beischel, and Van Anders (2024).
29. Rosenberg et al. (2019).
30. Davy and Steinbock (2012).
31. Beischel et al. (2022).
32. Kai and Devor (2022).
33. Beischel et al. (2022).
34. Prunas (2019).
35. Ross et al. (2024).
36. Byers (2011).

37. Wilson et al. (2009).
38. Vidal-Ortiz (2002).
39. Robinson and Vidal-Ortiz (2013).
40. zamantakis (2023).
41. Billard (2019); Meyerowitz (2002).
42. Ahmed (2010).
43. Henry (2013); Park (2000).
44. Chuh (2003).
45. Lawson and Langdridge (2020); Wignall and McCormack (2017); Wignall et al. (2022).

4. t4t possibilities

1. Awkward-Rich and Malatino (2022).
2. Jones (2023).
3. Robinson and Moskowitz (2013); Robinson and Vidal-Ortiz (2013); Vidal-Ortiz and Robinson (2016).
4. Shadel (2018).
5. Awkward-Rich and Malatino (2022).
6. Awkward-Rich and Malatino (2022).
7. Malatino (2022).
8. Malatino (2020); Malatino (2022).
9. Adair and Aizura (2022).
10. Boi is a slang term within LGBTQ communities that can mean different things. One meaning of boi is a young trans man. Another meaning of boi is a trans man who is in early stages of transitioning.
11. Meyerowitz (2002).
12. Hsu (2022).
13. Robinson (2023).
14. Giwa and Greensmith (2012); Zamantakis (2020).
15. Zamantakis (2020).
16. Ussher et al. (2022).
17. Fernandez and Birnholtz (2019); Powell, Scott, and Henry (2020); Scheuerman, Branham, and Hamidi (2018).
18. Gamarel et al. (2022); Ussher et al. (2022).
19. Ward (2020).

20. zamantakis (2023).
21. Thompson (2018).
22. Serano (2007).
23. Gamarel et al. (2022).
24. Ussher et al. (2022).
25. Enszer (2016).
26. Combahee River Collective (1977).
27. Ashley (2024).
28. Ussher et al. (2022).
29. Malatino (2022).
30. Lundy-Harris (2022).
31. McPherson, Smith-Lovin, and Cook (2001).
32. Ward (2020).
33. Johnson (2016).
34. Gill-Peterson (2018).
35. Adair and Aizura (2022).
36. Kai and Devor (2022).
37. Marvin (2022).
38. Du Mont et al. (2021); Grant et al. (2011); Woods et al. (2013).
39. Marvin (2022).
40. Stearns (1995).
41. Hood (2020); Robinson (2023).
42. Adair and Aizura (2022).
43. Doorduin and Van Berlo (2014).
44. Gilbert (2020).
45. Edelman and Zimman (2014).
46. Malatino (2022).
47. Mallory (2022).
48. Robinson (2023).
49. Zaliznyak et al. (2023).

5. Gender Liberation and the Abolition of Sexual Identities

1. Sedgwick (1990).
2. Sedgwick (1990).
3. Foucault (1976).

4. Blank (2012); Foucault (1976); Katz (1995).
5. Foucault (1976).
6. To note, the history presented in this paragraph is very condensed, and race, class, location, and other social categories and processes deeply complicate this history. This paragraph is just giving a short overview of how homosexuality and sexual identities emerged in the twentieth century as a way to organize U.S. society.
7. Chauncey (1994); D'Emilio (1983).
8. Chauncey (1994).
9. Johnson (2004).
10. Canaday (2009).
11. Gould (2009).
12. Foucault (1976).
13. Sedgwick (1990); Stearns (1995).
14. Collins (2004); West and Zimmerman (1987).
15. Bey (2021); Sedgwick (1990); Stearns (1995).
16. Stearns (1995).
17. Cohen (1997).
18. Stotzer (2009); Ussher et al. (2022).
19. Dinno (2017); Lantz, Faulkner, and Mills (2024).
20. Westbrook (2020).
21. Ussher et al. (2022).
22. Stotzer (2009).
23. Albury et al. (2021); Fernandez and Birnholtz (2019).
24. Hendricks and Testa (2012); Tan et al. (2020); Testa et al. (2015).
25. Operario et al. (2008).
26. Ussher et al. (2022).
27. Enke (2012).
28. Collins (2004).
29. B.A. Robinson (2020a).
30. Butler (2004).
31. Galupo, Mitchell, and Davis (2015).
32. Thöni, Eisner, and Hässler (2024).
33. Davis et al. (2022).
34. Smith and Stanley (2011).

35. Westbrook and Schilt (2014).
36. B. A. Robinson (2020a).
37. Grant et al. (2011).
38. Davis et al. (2022).
39. B. A. Robinson (2020b); Smith and Stanley (2011).
40. Eastwood et al. (2021); B. A. Robinson (2020a).
41. Davis et al. (2022).
42. West and Zimmerman (1987).
43. Alexander (2023).
44. Bey (2022).
45. Patil (2022).
46. Miranda (2010); Morgensen (2010); Patil (2018); Patil (2022); Spillers (1987).
47. Gill-Peterson (2024).
48. Miranda (2010).
49. Arvin, Tuck, and Morrill (2013).
50. Morgensen (2010).
51. Oyěwùmí (1997).
52. Oyěwùmí (1997).
53. M. Robinson (2020).
54. Weil et al. (2023).
55. Adjepong (2023); Lugones (2007); Lugones (2008).
56. Adjepong (2023).
57. Westbrook (2020).
58. Shuster and Westbrook (2022).
59. Kirzinger et al. (2023).
60. Connell (1995); Rich (1980).
61. TallBear, Clarke, and Haraway (2018).
62. TallBear et al. (2018).
63. TallBear (2020).
64. TallBear (2020).
65. brown (2019).
66. Robinson and Vidal-Ortiz (2013).
67. Rich (1980); Ward (2020).

Methodological Appendix A

1. Billard and Zhang (2022).
2. Farber (2017).
3. Tompkins (2014).
4. Massanari (2017, 331).
5. Maxwell et al. (2020).
6. Auxier and Anderson (2021).
7. Taylor and Jackson (2018).
8. Charmaz (2006).
9. Deterding and Waters (2021).
10. Robinson and Vidal-Ortiz (2013); Ward (2008).
11. Taylor and Jackson (2018).
12. Church (1993).
13. Jones (2020).
14. Gray et al. (2020); Oliffe et al. (2021); Tungohan and Catungal (2022).
15. Charmaz (2006).
16. Deterding and Waters (2021).
17. brown (2019).
18. Robinson (2022).

References

Adair, Cassius, and Aren Aizura. 2022. "'The Transgender Craze Seducing Our [Sons]'; or, All the Trans Guys Are Just Dating Each Other." *TSQ: Transgender Studies Quarterly* 9(1):44–64.

Adjepong, Anima. 2020. "Voetsek! Get[ting] Lost: African Sportswomen in 'the Sporting Black Diaspora.'" *International Review for the Sociology of Sport* 55(7):868–83.

Adjepong, Anima. 2023. "Queer African Feminist Orientations for a Trans Sports Studies." *TSQ: Transgender Studies Quarterly* 10(2):153–59.

Ahmed, Sara. 2010. *The Promise of Happiness*. Durham, NC: Duke University Press.

Albury, Kath, Christopher Dietzel, Tinonee Pym, Son Vivienne, and Teddy Cook. 2021. "Not Your Unicorn: Trans Dating App Users' Negotiations of Personal Safety and Sexual Health." *Health Sociology Review* 30(1):72–86.

Alexander, Qui Dorian. 2023. "TERF Logics Are Carceral Logics: Toward the Abolition of Gender-Critical Movements or Black Trans Life as Pedagogical Praxis." *Women's Studies in Communication* 46(2):230–34.

Anzani, Annalisa, Louis Lindley, Giacomo Tognasso, M. Paz Galupo, and Antonio Prunas. 2021. "'Being Talked to Like I Was a Sex Toy, Like Being Transgender Was Simply for the Enjoyment of Someone Else': Fetishization and Sexualization of Transgender and Nonbinary Individuals." *Archives of Sexual Behavior* 50(3):897–911.

Arvin, Maile, Eve Tuck, and Angie Morrill. 2013. "Decolonizing Feminism: Challenging Connections Between Settler Colonialism and Heteropatriarchy." *Feminist Formations* 25(1):8–34.

Ashley, Florence. 2024. *Gender/Fucking*. Troy, NY: CLASH Books.
Austin, Ashley, Ryan Papciak, and Lindsay Lovins. 2022. "Gender Euphoria: A Grounded Theory Exploration of Experiencing Gender Affirmation." *Psychology & Sexuality* 13(5):1406–26.
Auxier, Brooke, and Monica Anderson. 2021. "Social Media Use in 2021." *Pew Research Center: Internet, Science & Tech*, April 7 (www.pewresearch.org/internet/2021/04/07/social-media-use-in-2021/).
Awkward-Rich, Cameron, and Hil Malatino. 2022. "Meanwhile, t4t." *TSQ: Transgender Studies Quarterly* 9(1):1–8.
Beischel, Will J., Stéphanie E. M. Gauvin, and Sari M. Van Anders. 2022. "'A Little Shiny Gender Breakthrough': Community Understandings of Gender Euphoria." *International Journal of Transgender Health* 23(3):274–94.
Bey, Marquis. 2021. *Black Trans Feminism*. Durham, NC: Duke University Press.
Bey, Marquis. 2022. *Cistem Failure: Essays on Blackness and Cisgender*. Durham, NC: Duke University Press.
Billard, Thomas J. 2019. "'Passing' and the Politics of Deception: Transgender Bodies, Cisgender Aesthetics, and the Policing of Inconspicuous Marginal Identities." Pp. 463–77 in *The Palgrave Handbook of Deceptive Communication*, edited by T. Docan-Morgan. Cham, Switzerland: Springer International Publishing.
Billard, Thomas J., and Erique Zhang. 2022. "Toward a Transgender Critique of Media Representation." *JCMS: Journal of Cinema and Media Studies* 61(2):194–99.
Blair, Karen L., and Rhea Ashley Hoskin. 2019. "Transgender Exclusion from the World of Dating: Patterns of Acceptance and Rejection of Hypothetical Trans Dating Partners as a Function of Sexual and Gender Identity." *Journal of Social and Personal Relationships* 36(7):2074–95.
Blank, Hanne. 2012. *Straight: The Surprisingly Short History of Heterosexuality*. Boston: Beacon Press.
Bonilla-Silva, Eduardo. 2003. *Racism Without Racists: Color-Blind Racism and the Persistence of Racial Inequality in the United States*. Lanham, MD: Rowman & Littlefield.
Broussard, Kristin A., and Ruth H. Warner. 2019. "Gender Nonconformity Is Perceived Differently for Cisgender and Transgender Targets." *Sex Roles* 80(7):409–28.

brown, adrienne maree. 2019. *Pleasure Activism: The Politics of Feeling Good.* Chico, CA: AK Press.

Buggs, Shantel Gabrieal. 2020. "(Dis)Owning Exotic: Navigating Race, Intimacy, and Trans Identity." *Sociological Inquiry* 90(2): 249–70.

Burns, Jason A., Will J. Beischel, and Sari M. Van Anders. 2024. "Hormone Therapy and Trans Sexuality: A Review." *Psychology of Sexual Orientation and Gender Diversity* 11(1):17–30.

Butler, Judith. 1990. *Gender Trouble: Feminism and the Subversion of Identity.* New York: Routledge.

Butler, Judith. 2004. *Undoing Gender.* New York: Routledge.

Byers, E. Sandra. 2011. "Beyond the Birds and the Bees and Was It Good for You?: Thirty Years of Research on Sexual Communication." *Canadian Psychology / Psychologie Canadienne* 52(1):20–28.

Cambridge Dictionary. 2025. "Comfort." Retrieved February 25, 2025 (https://dictionary.cambridge.org/us/dictionary/english/comfort).

Canaday, Margot. 2009. *The Straight State: Sexuality and Citizenship in Twentieth-Century America.* Princeton, NJ: Princeton University Press.

Carlström, Rebeccah, Susanna Ek, and Sebastian Gabrielsson. 2021. "'Treat Me with Respect': Transgender Persons' Experiences of Encounters with Healthcare Staff." *Scandinavian Journal of Caring Sciences* 35(2): 600–607.

Chadwick, Sara B., and Sari M. van Anders. 2017. "Do Women's Orgasms Function as a Masculinity Achievement for Men?" *Journal of Sex Research* 54(9):1141–52.

Chamberland, Alex Alvina. 2016. "Femininity in Transgender Studies." *Lambda Nordica* 21(1–2):107–33.

Charmaz, Kathy. 2006. *Constructing Grounded Theory: A Practical Guide Through Qualitative Analysis.* Thousand Oaks, CA: Sage Publications.

Chauncey, George. 1994. *Gay New York: Gender, Urban Culture, and the Making of the Gay Male World, 1890–1940.* New York: Basic Books.

Cheney, Ann M. 2011. "'Most Girls Want to Be Skinny': Body (Dis)Satisfaction Among Ethnically Diverse Women." *Qualitative Health Research* 21(10):1347–59.

Chuh, Kandice. 2003. "Discomforting Knowledge: Or, Korean 'Comfort Women' and Asian Americanist Critical Practice." *Journal of Asian American Studies* 6(1):5–23.

Church, Allan H. 1993. "Estimating the Effect of Incentives on Mail Survey Response Rates: A Meta-Analysis." *Public Opinion Quarterly* 57(1):62–79.

Cohen, Cathy J. 1997. "Punks, Bulldaggers, and Welfare Queens: The Radical Potential of Queer Politics?" *GLQ: A Journal of Lesbian and Gay Studies* 3(4):437–65.

Collins, Patricia Hill. 1990. *Black Feminist Thought: Knowledge, Consciousness, and the Politics of Empowerment*. Boston: Unwin Hyman.

Collins, Patricia Hill. 2004. *Black Sexual Politics: African Americans, Gender, and the New Racism*. New York: Routledge.

Combahee River Collective. 1977. "A Black Feminist Statement."

Connell, R. W. 1995. *Masculinities*. Berkeley: University of California Press.

Costello, Cary Gabriel. 2021. "The 4chan '#SuperStraight' Troll Campaign." *Medium*, March 7 (https://transfusion.medium.com/the-4chan-super-straight-troll-campaign-ac99ef3b2fdb).

Cottom, Tressie McMillan. 2019. *Thick: And Other Essays*. New York: The New Press.

Davis, Angela Y. 1981. *Women, Race & Class*. New York: Random House.

Davis, Angela Y., Gina Dent, Erica R. Meiners, and Beth E. Richie. 2022. *Abolition. Feminism. Now*. Chicago: Haymarket Books.

Davy, Zowie, and Eliza Steinbock. 2012. "'Sexing Up' Bodily Aesthetics: Notes Towards Theorizing Trans Sexuality." Pp. 266–85 in *Sexualities: Past Reflections, Future Directions*, edited by S. Hines and Y. Taylor. London: Palgrave Macmillan.

Davy, Zowie, and Michael Toze. 2018. "What Is Gender Dysphoria? A Critical Systematic Narrative Review." *Transgender Health* 3(1):159–69.

D'Emilio, John. 1983. "Capitalism and Gay Identity." Pp. 100–113 in *Powers of Desire: The Politics of Sexuality*, edited by A. Snitow, C. Stansell, and S. Thompson. New York: Monthly Review Press.

Deterding, Nicole M., and Mary C. Waters. 2021. "Flexible Coding of In-Depth Interviews: A Twenty-First-Century Approach." *Sociological Methods & Research* 50(2):708–39.

Dinno, Alexis. 2017. "Homicide Rates of Transgender Individuals in the United States: 2010–2014." *American Journal of Public Health* 107(9):1441–47.

Doorduin, Tamar, and Willy Van Berlo. 2014. "Trans People's Experience of Sexuality in the Netherlands: A Pilot Study." *Journal of Homosexuality* 61(5):654-72.

DuBois, L. Zachary, and Heather Shattuck-Heidorn. 2021. "Challenging the Binary: Gender/Sex and the Bio-Logics of Normalcy." *American Journal of Human Biology* 33(5):e23623.

Du Mont, Janice, Sarah D. Kosa, Rebecca Abavi, Hannah Kia, and Sheila Macdonald. 2021. "Toward Affirming Care: An Initial Evaluation of a Sexual Violence Treatment Network's Capacity for Addressing the Needs of Trans Sexual Assault Survivors." *Journal of Interpersonal Violence* 36(21-22):NP12436-55.

Eastwood, Elizabeth A., Amanda J. Nace, Sabina Hirshfield, and Jeffrey M. Birnbaum. 2021. "Young Transgender Women of Color: Homelessness, Poverty, Childhood Sexual Abuse and Implications for HIV Care." *AIDS and Behavior* 25(1):96-106.

Edelman, Elijah Adiv, and Lal Zimman. 2014. "Boycunts and Bonus Holes: Trans Men's Bodies, Neoliberalism, and the Sexual Productivity of Genitals." *Journal of Homosexuality* 61(5):673-90.

Encyclopedia.com. 2025. "Comfort." Retrieved February 25, 2025 (www.encyclopedia.com/literature-and-arts/language-linguistics-and-literary-terms/english-vocabulary-d/comfort).

Encyclopedia.com. 2025. "Comfortable." Retrieved February 25, 2025 (www.encyclopedia.com/humanities/dictionaries-thesauruses-pictures-and-press-releases/comfortable).

Enke, A. F. 2012. "The Education of Little Cis: Cisgender and the Discipline of Opposing Bodies." Pp. 60-77 in *Transfeminist Perspectives In and Beyond Transgender and Gender Studies*, edited by A. Enke. Philadelphia: Temple University Press.

Enszer, Julie R. 2016. "'How to Stop Choking to Death': Rethinking Lesbian Separatism as a Vibrant Political Theory and Feminist Practice." *Journal of Lesbian Studies* 20(2):180-96.

Espineira, Karine. 2016. "Transgender and Transsexual People's Sexuality in the Media." *Parallax* 22(3):323-29.

Farber, Rebecca. 2017. "'Transing' Fitness and Remapping Transgender Male Masculinity in Online Message Boards." *Journal of Gender Studies* 26(3):254-68.

Ferguson, Roderick A. 2003. *Aberrations in Black: Toward a Queer of Color Critique*. Minneapolis: University of Minnesota Press.

Fernandez, Julia R., and Jeremy Birnholtz. 2019. "'I Don't Want Them to Not Know': Investigating Decisions to Disclose Transgender Identity on Dating Platforms." *Proceedings of the ACM on Human-Computer Interaction* 3(CSCW):1–21.

Forbes, TehQuin D., and Lawrence Stacey. 2022. "Personal Preferences, Discursive Strategies, and the Maintenance of Inequality on Gay Dating Apps." *Archives of Sexual Behavior* 51(5):2385–97.

Foucault, Michel. (1976) 1990. *The History of Sexuality, Volume 1: An Introduction*. Translated by R. Hurley. New York: Vintage Books.

Galupo, M. Paz, Shane B. Henise, and Nicholas L. Mercer. 2016. "'The Labels Don't Work Very Well': Transgender Individuals' Conceptualizations of Sexual Orientation and Sexual Identity." *International Journal of Transgenderism* 17(2):93–104.

Galupo, M. Paz, Renae C. Mitchell, and Kyle S. Davis. 2015. "Sexual Minority Self-Identification: Multiple Identities and Complexity." *Psychology of Sexual Orientation and Gender Diversity* 2(4):355–64.

Gamarel, Kristi E., Laura Jadwin-Cakmak, Wesley M. King, Ashley Lacombe-Duncan, Racquelle Trammell, Lilianna A. Reyes, Cierra Burks, Bré Rivera, Emily Arnold, and Gary W. Harper. 2022. "Stigma Experienced by Transgender Women of Color in Their Dating and Romantic Relationships: Implications for Gender-Based Violence Prevention Programs." *Journal of Interpersonal Violence* 37(9–10):NP8161–89.

Gercio, Hender. 2015. "Looking for That 'Special' Lady: Exploring Hegemonic Masculinity in Online Dating Profiles of Trans-Attracted Men." M.A. thesis, Central European University, Budapest, Hungary.

Gilbert, Aster. 2020. "Sissy Remixed." *TSQ: Transgender Studies Quarterly* 7(2):222–36.

Gill-Peterson, Jules. 2018. *Histories of the Transgender Child*. Minneapolis: University of Minnesota Press.

Gill-Peterson, Jules. 2024. *A Short History of Trans Misogyny*. New York: Verso Books.

Giwa, Sulaimon, and Cameron Greensmith. 2012. "Race Relations and Racism in the LGBTQ Community of Toronto: Perceptions of Gay and

Queer Social Service Providers of Color." *Journal of Homosexuality* 59(2):149–85.

Goffman, Erving. 1963. *Stigma: Notes on the Management of Spoiled Identity*. Englewood Cliffs, NJ: Prentice-Hall.

Gould, Deborah B. 2009. *Moving Politics: Emotion and ACT UP's Fight Against AIDS*. Chicago: University of Chicago Press.

Grant, Jaime, Lisa Mottet, Justin Tanis, and D. Min. 2011. "Injustice at Every Turn: A Report of the National Transgender Discrimination Survey." Washington, DC: National Center for Transgender Equality and National Gay and Lesbian Task Force.

Gray, Lisa, Gina Wong-Wylie, Gwen Rempel, and Karen Cook. 2020. "Expanding Qualitative Research Interviewing Strategies: Zoom Video Communications." *The Qualitative Report* 25(5):1292–1301.

Griffiths, Daniel A., and Heather L. Armstrong. 2023. "'They Were Talking to an Idea They Had About Me': A Qualitative Analysis of Transgender Individuals' Experiences Using Dating Apps." *Journal of Sex Research* 61(1):119–32.

Han, C. Winter. 2021. *Racial Erotics: Gay Men of Color, Sexual Racism, and the Politics of Desire*. Seattle: University of Washington Press.

Henderson, Kevin. 2020. "J. K. Rowling and the White Supremacist History of 'Biological Sex.'" *The Abusable Past*, July 28 (https://abusablepast.org/j-k-rowling-and-the-white-supremacist-history-of-biological-sex/).

Hendricks, Michael L., and Rylan J. Testa. 2012. "A Conceptual Framework for Clinical Work with Transgender and Gender Nonconforming Clients: An Adaptation of the Minority Stress Model." *Professional Psychology: Research and Practice* 43(5):460–67.

Henry, Nicola. 2013. "Memory of an Injustice: The 'Comfort Women' and the Legacy of the Tokyo Trial." *Asian Studies Review* 37(3):362–80.

Holland, Sharon Patricia. 2012. *The Erotic Life of Racism*. Durham, NC: Duke University Press.

Hood, Jamie. 2020. "Against Discourse: The Chaser Myth & the Un/Making of a Modern Woman." *TSQ*Now*, August 3 (www.tsqnow.online/post/against-discourse-the-chaser-myth-the-un-making-of-a-modern-woman-by-jamie-hood).

Hsu, V. Jo. 2022. "T4t Love-Politics." *TSQ: Transgender Studies Quarterly* 9(1):101–18.

Jagose, Annamarie. 1996. *Queer Theory: An Introduction*. New York: NYU Press.

Jarne, Philippe, and Josh R. Auld. 2006. "Animals Mix It Up Too: The Distribution of Self-Fertilization Among Hermaphroditic Animals." *Evolution* 60(9):1816–24.

Johns, Michelle Marie, Emily Pingel, Anna Eisenberg, Matthew Leslie Santana, and José Bauermeister. 2012. "Butch Tops and Femme Bottoms? Sexual Positioning, Sexual Decision Making, and Gender Roles Among Young Gay Men." *American Journal of Men's Health* 6(6):505–18.

Johnson, Austin. 2016. "Transnormativity: A New Concept and Its Validation Through Documentary Film About Transgender Men." *Sociological Inquiry* 86(4):465–91.

Johnson, David K. 2004. *The Lavender Scare: The Cold War Persecution of Gays and Lesbians in the Federal Government*. Chicago: University of Chicago Press.

Jones, Angela. 2019. "Sex Is Not a Problem: The Erasure of Pleasure in Sexual Science Research." *Sexualities* 22(4):643–68.

Jones, Angela. 2020. *Camming: Money, Power, and Pleasure in the Sex Work Industry*. New York: NYU Press.

Jones, Angela. 2023. "'It's Hard Out Here for a Unicorn': Transmasculine and Nonbinary Escorts, Embodiment, and Inequalities in Cisgendered Workplaces." *Gender & Society* 37(5):665–98.

Kai, Jacobsen, and Aaron Devor. 2022. "Moving from Gender Dysphoria to Gender Euphoria: Trans Experiences of Positive Gender-Related Emotions." *Bulletin of Applied Transgender Studies* 1(1–2):119–43.

Katz, Jonathan. 1995. *The Invention of Heterosexuality*. Chicago: University of Chicago Press.

Kil, Sang Hea. 2012. "Fearing Yellow, Imagining White: Media Analysis of the Chinese Exclusion Act of 1882." *Social Identities* 18(6):663–77.

Kirzinger, Ashley, Audrey Kearney, Alex Montero, Grace Sparks, Lindsey Dawson, and Mollyann Brodie. 2023. "KFF/The Washington Post Trans Survey." *KFF*, March 24 (www.kff.org/report-section/kff-the-washington-post-trans-survey-trans-in-america/).

Koch-Rein, Anson, Elahe Haschemi Yekani, and Jasper J. Verlinden. 2020. "Representing Trans: Visibility and Its Discontents." *European Journal of English Studies* 24(1):1–12.

Krell, Elías Cosenza. 2017. "Is Transmisogyny Killing Trans Women of Color? Black Trans Feminisms and the Exigencies of White Femininity." *TSQ: Transgender Studies Quarterly* 4(2):226-42.

Lantz, Brendan, Lexi Faulkner, and Jack M. Mills. 2024. "A Descriptive Account of the Nature and Extent of Transgender Homicide in America, 2010 to 2021." *Journal of Interpersonal Violence* 39(1-2):341-68.

Lawson, Jamie, and Darren Langdridge. 2020. "History, Culture and Practice of Puppy Play." *Sexualities* 23(4):574-91.

Lugones, María. 2007. "Heterosexualism and the Colonial/Modern Gender System." *Hypatia* 22(1):186-219.

Lugones, María. 2008. "The Coloniality of Gender." *Worlds & Knowledges Otherwise* 2:1-17.

Lundy-Harris, Amira. 2022. "'Necessary Bonding': On Black Trans Studies, Kinship, and Black Feminist Genealogies." *TSQ: Transgender Studies Quarterly* 9(1):84-100.

Malatino, Hil. 2020. *Trans Care*. Minneapolis: University of Minnesota Press.

Malatino, Hil. 2022. *Side Affects: On Being Trans and Feeling Bad*. Minneapolis: University of Minnesota Press.

Mallory, Allen B. 2022. "Dimensions of Couples' Sexual Communication, Relationship Satisfaction, and Sexual Satisfaction: A Meta-Analysis." *Journal of Family Psychology* 36(3):358-71.

Marvin, Amy. 2022. "Short-Circuited Trans Care, t4t, and Trans Scenes." *TSQ: Transgender Studies Quarterly* 9(1):9-27.

Massanari, Adrienne. 2017. "#Gamergate and The Fappening: How Reddit's Algorithm, Governance, and Culture Support Toxic Technocultures." *New Media & Society* 19(3):329-46.

Maxwell, December, Sarah R. Robinson, Jessica R. Williams, and Craig Keaton. 2020. "'A Short Story of a Lonely Guy': A Qualitative Thematic Analysis of Involuntary Celibacy Using Reddit." *Sexuality & Culture* 24(6):1852-74.

McLaughlin, J. F., Kinsey M. Brock, Isabella Gates, Anisha Pethkar, Marcus Piattoni, Alexis Rossi, and Sara E. Lipshutz. 2023. "Multivariate Models of Animal Sex: Breaking Binaries Leads to a Better Understanding of Ecology and Evolution." *Integrative and Comparative Biology* 63(4):891-906.

McPherson, Miller, Lynn Smith-Lovin, and James M. Cook. 2001. "Birds of a Feather: Homophily in Social Networks." *Annual Review of Sociology* 27(1):415-44.

Meyerowitz, Joanne. 2002. *How Sex Changed: A History of Transsexuality in the United States*. Cambridge, MA: Harvard University Press.

Miranda, Deborah A. 2010. "Extermination of the Joyas: Gendercide in Spanish California." *GLQ: A Journal of Lesbian and Gay Studies* 16(1-2):253-84.

Morgensen, Scott Lauria. 2010. "Settler Homonationalism: Theorizing Settler Colonialism Within Queer Modernities." *GLQ: A Journal of Lesbian and Gay Studies* 16(1-2):105-31.

Muro, Jazmín A., and Lisa M. Martinez. 2016. "Constrained Desires: The Romantic Partner Preferences of College-Educated Latinas." *Latino Studies* 14(2):172-91.

Oliffe, John L., Mary T. Kelly, Gabriela Gonzalez Montaner, and Wellam F. Yu Ko. 2021. "Zoom Interviews: Benefits and Concessions." *International Journal of Qualitative Methods* 20:16094069211053522.

Operario, Don, Jennifer Burton, Kristen Underhill, and Jae Sevelius. 2008. "Men Who Have Sex with Transgender Women: Challenges to Category-Based HIV Prevention." *AIDS and Behavior* 12(1):18-26.

Orne, Jason. 2017. *Boystown: Sex and Community in Chicago*. Chicago: University of Chicago Press.

Oyěwùmí, Oyèrónké. 1997. *The Invention of Women: Making an African Sense of Western Gender Discourses*. Minneapolis: University of Minnesota Press.

Painter, Nell Irvin. 1996. *Sojourner Truth: A Life, a Symbol*. New York: W. W. Norton & Company.

Park, You-Me. 2000. "Comforting the Nation: 'Comfort Women,' the Politics of Apology and the Workings of Gender." *Interventions* 2(2):199-211.

Patil, Vrushali. 2018. "The Heterosexual Matrix as Imperial Effect." *Sociological Theory* 36(1):1-26.

Patil, Vrushali. 2022. *Webbed Connectivities: The Imperial Sociology of Sex, Gender, and Sexuality*. Minneapolis: University of Minnesota Press.

Powell, Anastasia, Adrian J. Scott, and Nicola Henry. 2020. "Digital Harassment and Abuse: Experiences of Sexuality and Gender Minority Adults." *European Journal of Criminology* 17(2):199-223.

Prunas, A. 2019. "The Pathologization of Trans-Sexuality: Historical Roots and Implications for Sex Counselling with Transgender Clients." *Sexologies* 28(3):e54–60.

Puckett, Jae A., Kalei Glozier, Devon Kimball, and Rowan Giffel. 2021. "A Systematic Review of Sexuality Measurement in Transgender and Gender Diverse Populations." *Psychology of Sexual Orientation and Gender Diversity* 8(3):276–91.

Reisner, Sari L., Soon Kyu Choi, Jody L. Herman, Walter Bockting, Evan A. Krueger, and Ilan H. Meyer. 2023. "Sexual Orientation in Transgender Adults in the United States." *BMC Public Health* 23(1):1799.

Rich, Adrienne. 1980. "Compulsory Heterosexuality and Lesbian Existence." *Signs* 5(4):631–60.

Robinson, Brandon Andrew. 2015. "'Personal Preference' as the New Racism: Gay Desire and Racial Cleansing in Cyberspace." *Sociology of Race and Ethnicity* 1(2):317–30.

Robinson, Brandon Andrew. 2020a. *Coming Out to the Streets: LGBTQ Youth Experiencing Homelessness*. Oakland: University of California Press.

Robinson, Brandon Andrew. 2020b. "The Lavender Scare in Homonormative Times: Policing, Hyper-Incarceration, and LGBTQ Youth Homelessness." *Gender & Society* 34(2):210–32.

Robinson, Brandon Andrew. 2022. "Non-Binary Embodiment, Queer Knowledge Production, and Disrupting the Cisnormative Field: Notes from a Trans Ethnographer." *Journal of Men's Studies* 30(3):425–45.

Robinson, Brandon Andrew. 2023. "Transamorous Misogyny: Masculinity, Heterosexuality, and Cis Men's Sexist Desires for Trans Women." *Men and Masculinities* 26(3):356–75.

Robinson, Brandon Andrew. 2024. "Super Straights: Heterosexuality, White Supremacy, and Transphobia Without Transphobes." *Bulletin of Applied Transgender Studies* 3(1–2):137–57.

Robinson, Brandon Andrew, and David A. Moskowitz. 2013. "The Eroticism of Internet Cruising as a Self-Contained Behaviour: A Multivariate Analysis of Men Seeking Men Demographics and Getting Off Online." *Culture, Health & Sexuality* 15(5):555–69.

Robinson, Brandon Andrew, and Salvador Vidal-Ortiz. 2013. "Displacing the Dominant 'Down Low' Discourse: Deviance, Same-Sex Desire, and Craigslist.Org." *Deviant Behavior* 34(3):224–41.

Robinson, Margaret. 2020. "Two-Spirit Identity in a Time of Gender Fluidity." *Journal of Homosexuality* 67(12):1675–90.

Rosenberg, Shoshana, P. J. Matt Tilley, and Julia Morgan. 2019. "'I Couldn't Imagine My Life Without It': Australian Trans Women's Experiences of Sexuality, Intimacy, and Gender-Affirming Hormone Therapy." *Sexuality & Culture* 23(3):962–77.

Ross, Maeghan, Pip Roijer, Margriet Mullender, and Tim C. Van De Grift. 2024. "Trans, Gender Non-Conforming and Non-Binary Individuals' Perspectives on Experienced Sexuality During Medical Transition." *Journal of Sex & Marital Therapy* 50(3):379–394.

Scheuerman, Morgan Klaus, Stacy M. Branham, and Foad Hamidi. 2018. "Safe Spaces and Safe Places: Unpacking Technology-Mediated Experiences of Safety and Harm with Transgender People." *Proceedings of the ACM on Human-Computer Interaction* 2(CSCW):1–27.

Schilt, Kristen. 2015. "Born This Way: Thinking Sociologically About Essentialism." Pp. 1–14 in *Emerging Trends in the Social and Behavioral Sciences*, edited by R. A. Scott and S. M. Kosslyn. Hoboken, NJ: Wiley.

Schilt, Kristen, and Danya Lagos. 2017. "The Development of Transgender Studies in Sociology." *Annual Review of Sociology* 43:425–43.

Schilt, Kristen, and Laurel Westbrook. 2009. "Doing Gender, Doing Heteronormativity: 'Gender Normals,' Transgender People, and the Social Maintenance of Heterosexuality." *Gender & Society* 23(4):440–64.

Sedgwick, Eve Kosofsky. 1990. *Epistemology of the Closet*. Berkeley: University of California Press.

Serano, Julia. 2007. *Whipping Girl: A Transsexual Woman on Sexism and the Scapegoating of Femininity*. New York: Seal Press.

Serano, Julia. 2024. "Why Are 'Gender Critical' Activists So Fond of Gametes?" *Switch Hitter*, February 12 (https://juliaserano.substack.com/p/why-are-gender-critical-activists).

Shadel, Jon. 2018. "As Craigslist Personal Ads Shut Down, We're Losing an Important Queer Space." *Washington Post*, March 27.

Shuster, Stef M., and Laurel Westbrook. 2022. "Reducing the Joy Deficit in Sociology: A Study of Transgender Joy." *Social Problems* 71(3):791–809.

Smilges, J. Logan. 2020. "On Being a Remarkable Trans." *TSQ*Now*, December 17 (www.tsqnow.online/post/on-being-a-remarkable-trans).

Smith, Nat, and Eric A. Stanley. 2011. *Captive Genders: Trans Embodiment and the Prison Industrial Complex.* Chico, CA: AK Press.

Somerville, Siobhan B. 2000. *Queering the Color Line: Race and the Invention of Homosexuality in American Culture.* Durham, NC: Duke University Press.

Spillers, Hortense J. 1987. "Mama's Baby, Papa's Maybe: An American Grammar Book." *Diacritics* 17(2):64–81.

Stearns, Deborah C. 1995. "Gendered Sexuality: The Privileging of Sex and Gender in Sexual Orientation." *NWSA Journal* 7(1):8–29.

Steinbugler, Amy C. 2012. *Beyond Loving: Intimate Racework in Lesbian, Gay, and Straight Interracial Relationships.* Oxford: Oxford University Press.

Stember, Charles Herbert. 1978. *Sexual Racism: The Emotional Barrier to an Integrated Society.* New York: Harper & Row.

Stotzer, Rebecca L. 2009. "Violence Against Transgender People: A Review of United States Data." *Aggression and Violent Behavior* 14(3):170–79.

Strings, Sabrina. 2019. *Fearing the Black Body: The Racial Origins of Fat Phobia.* New York: NYU Press.

Sumerau, J. E., Ryan T. Cragun, and Lain A. B. Mathers. 2016. "Contemporary Religion and the Cisgendering of Reality." *Social Currents* 3(3):293–311.

Sumerau, J. E., and Lain A. B. Mathers. 2019. *America Through Transgender Eyes.* Lanham, MA: Rowman & Littlefield.

TallBear, Kim. 2020. "Identity Is a Poor Substitute for Relating: Genetic Ancestry, Critical Polyamory, Property, and Relations." Pp. 467–78 in *Routledge Handbook of Critical Indigenous Studies*, edited by B. Hokowhitu, A. Moreton-Robinson, L. Tuhiwai-Smith, C. Andersen, and S. Larkin. New York: Routledge.

TallBear, Kim, A. E. Clarke, and D. J. Haraway. 2018. "Making Love and Relations Beyond Settler Sex and Family." Pp. 18–28 in *Queerly Canadian: An Introductory Reader in Sexuality Studies*, edited by S. Rayter and L. Halpern Zisman. Toronto: Canadian Scholars' Press.

Tan, Kyle K. H., Gareth J. Treharne, Sonja J. Ellis, Johanna M. Schmidt, and Jaimie F. Veale. 2020. "Gender Minority Stress: A Critical Review." *Journal of Homosexuality* 67(10):1471–89.

Taylor, Kris, and Sue Jackson. 2018. "'I Want That Power Back': Discourses of Masculinity Within an Online Pornography Abstinence Forum." *Sexualities* 21(4):621–39.

Testa, Rylan J., Janice Habarth, Jayme Peta, Kimberly Balsam, and Walter Bockting. 2015. "Development of the Gender Minority Stress and Resilience Measure." *Psychology of Sexual Orientation and Gender Diversity* 2(1):65–77.

Thompson, Laura. 2018. "'I Can Be Your Tinder Nightmare': Harassment and Misogyny in the Online Sexual Marketplace." *Feminism & Psychology* 28(1):69–89.

Thöni, Cynthia, Leïla Eisner, and Tabea Hässler. 2024. "Not Straight Enough, nor Queer Enough: Identity Denial, Stigmatization, and Negative Affect Among Bisexual and Pansexual People." *Psychology of Sexual Orientation and Gender Diversity* 11(2):237–49.

Tompkins, Avery Brooks. 2014. "'There's No Chasing Involved': Cis/Trans Relationships, 'Tranny Chasers,' and the Future of a Sex-Positive Trans Politics." *Journal of Homosexuality* 61(5):766–80.

Truth, Sojourner. 1851. "Ain't I a Woman?"

Tungohan, Ethel, and John Paul Catungal. 2022. "Virtual Qualitative Research Using Transnational Feminist Queer Methodology: The Challenges and Opportunities of Zoom-Based Research During Moments of Crisis." *International Journal of Qualitative Methods* 21:16094069221090062.

Turley, Emma L., Surya Monro, and Nigel King. 2017. "Adventures of Pleasure: Conceptualising Consensual Bondage, Discipline, Dominance and Submission, and Sadism and Masochism as a Form of Adult Play." *International Journal of Play* 6(3):324–34.

Ussher, Jane M., Alexandra Hawkey, Janette Perz, Pranee Liamputtong, Jessica Sekar, Brahmaputra Marjadi, Virginia Schmied, Tinashe Dune, and Eloise Brook. 2022. "Crossing Boundaries and Fetishization: Experiences of Sexual Violence for Trans Women of Color." *Journal of Interpersonal Violence* 37(5–6):NP3552–84.

Velocci, Beans. 2024. "The History of Sex Research: Is 'Sex' a Useful Category?" *Cell* 187(6):1343–46.

Vidal-Ortiz, Salvador. 2002. "Queering Sexuality and Doing Gender: Transgender Men's Identification with Gender and Sexuality." Pp. 181–233 in *Gendered Sexualities*, edited by P. Gagné and R. Tewksbury. Leeds, UK: Emerald Group Publishing Limited.

Vidal-Ortiz, Salvador, and Brandon Andrew Robinson. 2016. "The Racial and Sexual Stereotypes of the 'Down Low' on Craigslist.Org." Pp. 353–62 in

Introducing the New Sexuality Studies, edited by N. L. Fischer and S. Seidman. New York: Routledge.

Vidal-Ortiz, Salvador, Brandon Andrew Robinson, and Cristina Khan. 2018. *Race and Sexuality*. Cambridge, UK: Polity Press.

Walters, Suzanna Danuta. 2014. *The Tolerance Trap: How God, Genes, and Good Intentions Are Sabotaging Gay Equality*. New York: NYU Press.

Ward, Jane. 2008. "Dude-Sex: White Masculinities and 'Authentic' Heterosexuality Among Dudes Who Have Sex with Dudes." *Sexualities* 11(4):414–34.

Ward, Jane. 2012. "Born This Way: Congenital Heterosexuals and the Making of Heteroflexibility." Pp. 91–108 in *Sexualities: Past Reflections, Future Directions, Genders and Sexualities in the Social Sciences*, edited by S. Hines and Y. Taylor. London: Palgrave Macmillan.

Ward, Jane. 2020. *The Tragedy of Heterosexuality*. New York: NYU Press.

Ward, Jane. 2021. "Heterosexuality." Pp. 113–16 in *Keywords for Gender and Sexuality Studies*, edited by The Keywords Feminist Editorial Collective. New York: NYU Press.

Weil, Abraham B., Camilah G. Hicks, Victor Ultra Omni, and Lady Dane Figueroa Edidi. 2023. "'Freer Than We Want to Be': On Marquis Bey's *Black Trans Feminism*." *The Black Scholar* 53(3-4):98–116.

West, Candace, and Don H. Zimmerman. 1987. "Doing Gender." *Gender & Society* 1(2):125–51.

Westbrook, Laurel. 2020. *Unlivable Lives: Violence and Identity in Transgender Activism*. Oakland: University of California Press.

Westbrook, Laurel, and Kristen Schilt. 2014. "Doing Gender, Determining Gender: Transgender People, Gender Panics, and the Maintenance of the Sex/Gender/Sexuality System." *Gender & Society* 28(1):32–57.

White, Deborah Gray. 1985. *Ar'n't I a Woman?: Female Slaves in the Plantation South*. New York: Norton.

Wignall, Liam, and Mark McCormack. 2017. "An Exploratory Study of a New Kink Activity: 'Pup Play.'" *Archives of Sexual Behavior* 46(3):801–11.

Wignall, Liam, Mark McCormack, Taylor Cook, and Rusi Jaspal. 2022. "Findings from a Community Survey of Individuals Who Engage in Pup Play." *Archives of Sexual Behavior* 51(7):3637–46.

Wilson, Patrick A., Pamela Valera, Ana Ventuneac, Ivan Balan, Matt Rowe, and Alex Carballo-Diéguez. 2009. "Race-Based Sexual Stereotyping and

Sexual Partnering Among Men Who Use the Internet to Identify Other Men for Bareback Sex." *Journal of Sex Research* 46(5):399–413.

Woods, Jordan Blair, Frank H. Galvan, Mohsen Bazargan, Jody L. Herman, and Ying-Tung Chen. 2013. "Latina Transgender Women's Interactions with Law Enforcement in Los Angeles County." *Policing: A Journal of Policy and Practice* 7(4):379–91.

Zaliznyak, Michael, Marie Lauzon, Jenna Stelmar, Nance Yuan, Shannon M. Smith, and Maurice M. Garcia. 2023. "Effects of Gender-Affirming Hormone Therapy on Orgasm Function of Transgender Men and Women: A Long Term Follow Up." *Urology* 174:86–91.

Zamantakis, Alithia. 2020. "Queering Intimate Emotions: Trans/Nonbinary People Negotiating Emotional Expectations in Intimate Relationships." *Sexualities* 25(5–6):581–97.

zamantakis, alithia. 2023. *Thinking Cis: Cisgender, Heterosexual Men, and Queer Women's Roles in Anti-Trans Violence*. Lanham, MA: Rowman & Littlefield.

Index

4chan, 35

abolition feminism, 111–13
abolition of sexual identities, 98–124
aggression, 77–79; racialized, 11
AIDS crisis, 100
anal sex, 55, 102
anti-Blackness, 33
asexuals, 2, 102
Asian people, 12, 21, 35, 56, 59, 66–67
assolf_shitler, 43–44
attraction, 16, 62, 65, 67, 98, 123, 137; and cisness, 20; and fetishization, 9, 79; and sexual cissexism, 24–26, 29, 34–44; sexual identities limiting, 101–2, 107–11; and sexual orientation, 2, 64, 101–2; and sexual racism, 21; and t4t, 82, 86; and transphobia, 34–44, 77

babno, 41
beauty norms, 26, 51
Bella, 78, 87
binary, 24, 51, 54; gender binary, 2–3, 6–8, 16, 36, 45, 56, 79, 85–86, 89–90, 98, 109–10, 114–20; homo/hetero binary, 6, 39, 110–11; sex binary, 6, 37–39, 41, 45, 56
biological essentialism, 26–29, 36–45. *See also* gender essentialism
biological sex, 37–39, 41
bisexuals, 2–3, 6, 62, 66, 100, 110–11, 122
Black men, 21, 33, 56, 62
Black people, 10–13, 15–16, 32–33, 61, 76, 113
Black women, 10–11, 75, 103, 106, 112
blowjobs, 94–95
bondage, 56–57
Bonilla-Silva, Eduardo, 38
"born this way" discourse, 41–44
bottoming, 12, 47, 55–58, 85
Bumble, 30

California, 117, 130; Alameda, 75; Berkeley, 63; Claremont, 76; Goleta, 61; Riverside, 5, 56, 63; Santa Barbara, 59; Thousand Oaks, 83

[165]

care, 119, 121–23, 125–26, 128, 131; and comfort, 13, 49, 59, 61; and t4t, 14, 73, 94–95, 97, 131
Carmen, 50–56, 58–59, 62–63, 65, 66, 81, 93
chasers, 9, 23–24, 30–31, 127
Chic, 62–63, 68–71, 114
Chinese women, 21
chromosomes, 37–38
cishet, definition, 139n3
cishet men, 2–3, 9, 14, 16, 104, 109–10
cis men, 3, 16, 28–31, 40, 49, 51–52, 55, 58, 62–66, 79, 85, 91–92, 109–10
cisness, 42, 63, 101, 112, 121, 127; challenging, 13–14, 17, 49–50, 52, 73–75, 80–85, 110, 114, 122, 125–26; definition, 5–6; and gender dysphoria, 51, 65–66; and heterosexuality, 8–9, 17, 20, 23–31, 89, 94, 103, 108; racialized, 34, 106–7, 116; and sexual cissexism, 22, 45, 97; violence of, 11, 46, 90
cis women, 9, 24–25, 27–29, 40, 51, 53, 55, 82, 87, 106, 110, 120
class, 76–77, 88, 122, 146n6; and beauty norms, 26, 51; and femininity, 30, 34, 107; racialized, 26, 30, 34, 45, 51, 107
coalitional politics, 80, 100–101, 106, 113, 122
Cohen, Cathy, 101
Cold War, 100
Collins, Patricia Hill, 10
colonialism/imperialism, 36, 39, 67, 115–18
comfort, 12–13, 46–71, 81–82, 87, 89–90, 102, 110, 114, 121–26, 133

comfort women, 66–67
communication, 121–22; and comfort, 13, 47, 49, 52–53, 60–61, 68, 70, 73; sexual, 59–61, 95–96; and t4t, 68, 73, 82, 91–92, 94–96
community, 51, 132; beyond identity, 101–2, 115, 121, 124; gay, 56, 99–100; LGBTQ, 15, 144n10; and t4t, 14, 73, 76, 82, 87, 122, 125–26, 128, 133; trans, 48–49, 82, 87
compulsory heterosexuality, 42, 50, 52, 65–66, 75, 80, 82, 84, 100, 109–11, 115, 120, 123; and cisness, 8–9, 17, 20, 23–31, 89, 94, 103, 108; definition, 4–6; and trans femmes, 1–18
connection, 108, 124; and comfort, 13, 67, 121–22; and t4t, 14–15, 73, 76, 82, 84, 88, 90–92, 97
consent, 13, 49, 121, 123, 125, 130–31
controlling images, 11
COVID-19 pandemic, 23, 120, 223
Craigslist, 72–73, 96, 125
crossdressing, 9, 112

Dakota, 90–96
dating, 1, 5–12, 16, 23, 119, 122, 128–32, 135–36, 138; of cis people, 31–32, 54, 62; and comfort, 13, 49, 53–55, 58, 62, 64–66, 68–69; and danger, 79, 104–5; and heterosexuality, 3, 30–31; and sexual cissexism, 20–22, 31–35, 42–45; and sexual racism, 21; and t4t, 13–15, 46, 65–66, 68–69, 72–84, 86, 88, 91, 97; and transphobia, 30–31, 35
dating apps, 6, 30, 53, 129, 136. *See also* Bumble; Grindr; Hinge

decolonizing gender, 115-18, 120
Delilah, 98, 111, 113
DeltaMx, 41
desexualization, 10-11, 19
desire, 4, 62-63, 72, 98, 108, 114, 120, 123-24, 126-27, 131, 137; and comfort, 49; and fetishization, 19; and heterosexuality, 2-6, 9, 11-12, 15-16; and sexual cissexism, 20-45, 106; and sexual identity, 64, 99-103, 110-11, 113, 121; and t4t, 73, 80-94; trans desire, 5, 7-9, 17, 53, 82-94; and transphobia, 79
Diagnostic and Statistical Manual of Mental Disorders (DSM), 60, 100
discomfort, 53, 59, 63, 66
discrimination, 7, 23, 48, 107, 113, 124, 126; and biological essentialism, 40-42, 44; and sexual cissexism, 22, 103, 105; and sexual stereotypes, 11; and t4t, 77-78, 80, 83, 87
disrespect, 52-54
Dontwanttogooglethat, 41
doorknoob, 41
DorianMaximus, 37-38
down low, 53, 62, 122

education, 94; educating cis people, 14, 31-32, 52-53, 64, 84
Egyptian people, 76
Emily, 56-57, 85-86, 88-89, 112
Emma, 63-64, 117-18
eroticism, 32, 57, 70, 73, 79, 99; and comfort, 61, 67; and t4t, 86, 90, 92, 94-95, ; and transmisogyny, 28-29

ethics, 125; of interviewing, 128-31
eugenics, 36, 42
euphoria, 48-49, 54-55, 58, 119, 122, 124, 130
Euphoria (TV show), 15-17
Eurocentrism, 36, 116-18, 120

Faith, 103-11
Family, Housing, and Me Project, 130
femininity, 24, 51, 63-65, 68-69, 72, 118, 126-27, 139n1; beyond cisness, 3-4; and bottoming, 56, 58; expansive, 16-17; and heteronormativity, 82; hyper-, 9-10, 19-20, 22, 25-26; and misogyny paradox, 79; racialized, 16, 26, 30, 106-7; and t4t, 82-89. *See also* trans feminine people
feminism, 4-5, 35, 127; abolition, 111-13
femme men, 78-79
fetishization, 19, 137; and comfort, 53-55, 63-64; and sexual cissexism, 9-11, 24, 31, 33, 49; and sexual racism, 21, 106; and t4t, 14, 75-81, 90-93
finsexuals, 102
Florida: Gainesville, 19
FOSTA-SESTA, 72
Foucault, Michel, 99
fucking, 12, 21-22, 55-58, 73, 91
furries, 69

Gabrielle, 19, 30-34, 46
gametes, 38-39
gatekeepers, 3
gay men, 41, 56, 63-64, 102

gay people, 2, 42–43, 56, 88, 111, 122; and gender, 63–64, 101–2, 107–8, 117; pathologization of, 100. *See also* lesbians
gay rights, 41–43
gender-affirming healthcare, 3, 46, 60, 96
gender binary, 2–3, 6–8, 16, 36, 45, 56, 79, 85–86, 89–90, 98, 109–10, 114–20
gender dysphoria, 27, 48, 51, 59–61, 85, 94–95, 119
gender essentialism, 2, 5, 43, 80, 87, 101, 121. *See also* biological essentialism
gender exploration, 81, 85–86, 88, 112, 119–20, 123
gender-fluid people, 83–84
gender identity, definition, 2
gender liberation, 5, 18; and abolition of sexual identities, 98–124; and comfort, 13, 46, 49; compulsory heterosexuality threatening, 8, 17; sexual cissexism threatening, 22, 45
gender-nonconforming people, 75, 120
gender policing, 106–9, 113, 115
gender transition, 7, 27, 50, 53, 57, 68, 79, 93–96, 144n10
genitals, 12, 38, 59, 86, 93, 95, 107; cis *vs.* trans pleasure, 27, 50–52; decentering, 61, 94, 97; and dysphoria, 60; fetishization of, 31, 33, 106; and sexual identities, 2, 8, 24, 40–41, 98–99, 103, 110–11
Gen Z, 35, 110
Georgia: Atlanta, 69
ggtab, 37–40
girl dick, 93–94, 109

Grindr, 9, 30
Gutierrez, Stephanie, 130
gynosexuals, 102

heteronormativity, 82, 101; cis-, 65
heterosexuality, 49, 63, 98; abolition of, 102–3; challenges to, 13–15, 50, 52, 55, 57–58, 61, 80–83, 84, 126; and cisness, 8–9, 17, 20, 23–31, 34, 65–66, 74–75, 80–84, 89, 94, 103, 107–8, 129n3; compulsory, 1–18, 42, 50, 52, 65–66, 75, 80, 82, 84, 89, 100, 109–11, 115, 120, 123; invention of, 35–36, 99–100, 116; and misogyny, 78–79; racialized, 101, 116–17; and sexual cissexism, 23–45, 57; and sexual positioning, 55–57; and transphobia, 23–45, 77. *See also* straightness
Hinge, 30
Hitler, Adolf, 35
homophily, 83
homophobia: internalized, 30–31
homosexuality, 8, 42, 102, 108–11; invention of, 35–36, 99–100
hooking up, 7–11, 16, 30, 34, 62, 64, 72, 105, 109, 128, 131, 136–38; and comfort, 12, 49–50, 52–55, 58–59, 68; and racism, 32–33; and t4t, 46, 73–74, 78–81, 90–94
hookup apps, 9–10, 16, 30. *See also* Bumble; Grindr; Hinge
hormones, 26–27, 38–39, 50–51, 59, 68, 96; hormone replacement therapy (HRT), 68, 93–94
hyperfemininity, 9–10, 19–20, 22, 25–26
hypersexuality, 9–12, 19–28, 33, 61, 81, 105–6

[168] INDEX

identity, 6, 127, 130; abolition of, 98-124; and comfort, 54-55, 62-64; gay identity, 63-64, 88, 101-2, 122; gender identity, 2, 14, 37-38, 82, 85, 88, 110, 114-15, 119-20, 122, 129, 137; limitations of, 8, 101-2, 107-11; and respect, 54-55; and sexual cissexism, 11, 20, 22, 24, 31-32, 35-45; sexual identity, 2-3, 7, 11, 31, 35, 39-41, 99, 129, 137, 146n6; straight identity, 3, 24, 35, 37, 101; and t4t, 15, 73, 76-77, 81-82, 85-88
Imani, 1-5, 9-17, 115-17, 125
Indigenous people, 32
intersecting oppressions, 10-11, 33-34, 45, 77, 98, 106
intersex people, 38
intimacy, 40, 109-10; and dysphoria, 60; gendered, 12; racialized, 76; and t4t, 73-74, 80, 82, 90, 94-95
intimate partner violence, 78, 105
intracommunity violence, 87

Japanese military, 66-67
jezebel stereotype, 10-11
Jim Crow, 11, 36
joy, 66, 121-24, 130-32; of comfort, 69; of gender exploration, 119-20; of sexual exploration, 68, 71; in trans studies, 48-49
joyas, 116
Juanita, 119

kink, 19, 33, 70, 89, 94, 124
Korean women, 66
Kyle Royce, 35

Latinx people, 12, 62-63, 103, 113
lesbians, 2-5, 14, 41, 61, 80, 100

LibraryLass, 44
Lin, 63-64

m4m, 72
mammy stereotype, 10-22
masculinity, 7, 51, 65, 82-84, 86-89, 114-15, 123, 127; cishet, 25, 28-30; and misogyny, 78-79; racialized, 11, 106; and topping, 56-57. *See also* trans masculine people
Massachusetts: Boston, 119
mazotori, 40
methodology of book, 7-8, 125-33
Mexican people, 21, 106
Minnesota: Minneapolis, 98
misogyny, 5, 28, 112, 127; trans-, 77-80, 87, 98, 111, 113; transmisognynoir, 33. *See also* sexism
misogyny paradox, 78-79
Monica, 83-84, 86-87
monosexuality, 64, 88, 101
Morales, Shell, 130

Nazism, 35, 44
nonbinary people, 2, 13, 88, 107, 114-15, 120, 129
North Carolina: Greensboro, 1, 13
Nour, 76

objectification, 14, 19, 21-22, 24, 30-31, 34, 45, 53-55, 77, 79, 81, 90, 92, 106, 137
Ohio, 10, 120
orgasms, 27-28, 59, 61, 67, 90, 94-97, 122, 124
Oyěwùmí, Oyèrónkẹ́, 117

Pacyniak, Kori, 130
Page Act (1975), 21

Index [169]

pansexuals, 2–3, 6, 62, 66, 90, 102, 110–11
pathologization, 6, 43, 48, 60, 62, 100, 122
Patty, 69–71
penetration, 12, 55–56, 58–59, 70, 89
Pennsylvania: Pittsburgh, 69
personal preference: as transphobia, 43–45
Pew Research, 126
pleasure, 18, 23, 32, 119–24, 136–37; and comfort, 13, 46–71; heterosexuality limiting, 6, 8, 17, 29; identities limiting, 8, 102, 109–11, 113; pleasurable possibilities, 7–8, 58, 67–71, 90–97, 102; sexual, 29, 58–59, 62, 67, 92, 96–97, 110; and sexual cissexism, 20, 22, 45; and t4t, 75, 82, 90–97; of trans knowledge production, 131–33; and transmisogyny, 25, 29–30, 79; trans pleasure, 5, 8–9, 17, 27–28, 34, 45, 54, 67–71, 75, 82, 90–97, 125, 128, 130
policing, 111–13
pornography, 22, 26, 33, 106
prisons, 11, 21; abolishing, 112–13
Puerto Ricans, 50
pup play, 70–71

Queer Nation, 100
queer people, 42, 69, 72, 76, 87, 101, 107; as dating partners, 62–63; trans queer people, 2–3, 14, 62
queer theory, 8, 98
Quinn, 61

racism, 10–11, 32, 38–39, 44, 75, 76, 111, 113, 122; sexual, 21, 33–34, 45, 61, 106–7. *See also* anti-Blackness; white supremacy
r/ChasersRiseUp, 23, 127
reciprocity, 121, 130–32
Reddit, 6, 23, 35, 37, 40–41, 44, 126–27
rejection, sexual, 19–22, 44–45, 108
reproduction, 36–41, 99, 116
respect, 13, 46, 102, 121, 123; and comfort, 52–55, 69–70; and t4t, 73, 75, 77, 81–84, 95
Rich, Adrienne, 4–5
Rodriguez Pinto, Laura, 130

Sabi, 50, 59–61
safety, 46, 102, 105, 112, 115, 121–22, 124–26, 128, 131; and comfort, 47, 53–55; and sexual cissexism, 20; and t4t, 77–83, 86–87, 97
sapiosexuals, 102
Schafer, Hunter, 16
Schutzstaffel, 35
Sedgwick, Eve, 98
Semenya, Caster, 39
separatism: lesbian, 80; t4t as, 15, 80
sex drive, 26–27, 59, 99
sexism, 10, 30. *See also* misogyny; sexual cissexism
sexual cissexism, 9–11, 19; challenging, 45–46, 90, 92, 95–96; and dating, 30–34; definition, 20–23; and heterosexuality, 23–30, 57; and sexual racism, 106–7; and super straightness (SS), 34–45; violence of, 103–7
sexual communication, 59–61, 95–96
sexual exploration, 47, 57–61, 65, 68–71, 81, 86, 92, 102, 111, 123
sexual freedom, 8, 18, 46, 50, 102, 133

sexual identity, 7, 129, 137; abolition of, 98-124; and biological essentialism, 41; and comfort, 62-64; and gender essentialism, 2; and healthcare access, 3; invention of, 99, 146n6; racialized, 39; and sexual cissexism, 11, 20, 22, 24, 45; and t4t, 88; and transness, 40; and transphobia, 31, 35
sexualities studies: pleasure turn, 48-49
sexual labels, 6-7, 17, 64, 99, 114, 121, 123-24
sexual orientation, 8, 98; definition, 2
sexual racism, 11, 33-34, 45, 61, 106-7; definition, 21
sexual violence, 5, 53, 66-67, 87, 103-4, 105, 113; racialized, 11, 21
sex work, 21, 72, 100, 112
shame, 33, 41-42, 79, 108, 123
slavery, 10-11, 21, 36, 66-67, 116-17
social media, 4, 6, 35, 42, 126, 129, 136
sodomy, 112
solidarity, 73, 82, 129, 131, 133
Southeast Asian people, 59
Statista, 126
Stember, Charles, 21
stereotypes, 14, 83-84, 112; jezebel, 10-11; mammy, 10-11; racially gendered, 11, 21-22, 33, 44, 56-58, 61-62; sexual, 12-13, 20, 44, 55, 111; of trans women and femmes, 25, 27, 29, 105
stigma, 31, 41-42, 111, 128
straight men, 2, 9, 34-35, 40, 62, 64, 66, 108
straightness, 17, 62, 64, 88, 102, 120; invention of, 35-36; and misogyny, 24, 28; and queerness, 101; super (SS), 34-45; and transphobia, 24, 31, 34-45, 108; and womanhood, 1-3. *See also* heterosexuality
submissiveness, 12, 19-22, 29, 56, 127
superphobes, 41-42
super straightness (SS), 34-45

t4t (trans for trans), 40, 46; and comfort, 65-66, 68; complications of, 86-90, 122; and Craigslist, 72-74; and dating, 74-77; and discrimination, 77-78, 80, 83, 87; and femininity, 82-89; and gender exploration, 85-86, 112; as methodology, 125-33; pleasurable possibilities of, 90-97, 110; and safety, 77-80; as separatism, 15, 80; and shared experience, 83-85; and social media, 4; as way beyond heterosexuality, 13-15, 80-83
Tejanas, 119
Tennessee, 130; Memphis, 78
Texas, 51; Houston, 103-4
Tiana, 74-75, 77-82, 84
TikTok, 35
topping, 12, 47, 56-57, 85
transamorous men, 23-24, 126-27
trans bois, 74; definition, 144n10
trans feminine people, 65, 68, 83, 85-86
trans femmes, 22, 57, 103, 105, 112, 120, 127-32; and comfort, 49-50, 53-54, 62-63; and compulsory heterosexuality, 1-18; definition, 139n1; and sexual cissexism, 19-20, 23-25, 30, 34, 45, 106; stereotyping of, 27; and t4t, 72-75; 78-79, 84-85, 88, 90, 93

Index [171]

trans girls, 50, 93, 95
trans masculine people, 7, 46, 65, 83, 86–87, 107, 144n10
trans men, 7, 13
transmisogynoir, 33
transmisogyny, 77–80, 87, 98, 111, 113
transness, 6, 8, 19, 40, 85–86
transphobia, 10, 22, 33, 77–79, 98, 105, 112, 126; and "born this way" discourse, 41–43; internalized, 31, 57; and "personal preference," 43–45; and super straightness, 34–45
transsexuality, 60
trans studies, 24, 125, 127, 132–33; joy/euphoria turn, 48–49
trans women, 103, 105, 107–10, 112–13, 117, 120, 126–32, 136, 138; and comfort, 49–50, 53–57, 62–63; and compulsory heterosexuality, 1–18; and sexual cissexism, 19–20, 22–31, 34–45, 106; and t4t, 73, 75, 77–81, 84, 86–95
Truth, Sojourner, 10, 140n28
Twitter/X, 35, 129

Under_score-, 24–29, 34
ungendering, 11
University of California, Riverside, 5

vetting of partners, 78–79, 87
vulnerability, 7, 27, 47, 105, 119, 128

Ward, Jane, 35
Washington: Seattle, 90
white men, 10, 16, 35
white supremacy, 21, 36, 39, 44, 76, 80, 107, 115–17. *See also* anti-Blackness
white women, 10–11
Winnie, 57–58
Wisconsin: Madison, 57
World War II, 66

xenogender, 118
xenophobia, 22

YouTube, 3, 126

zamantakis, alithia, 6
Zendaya, 16
Zoom, 1, 98, 129–30

Founded in 1893,
UNIVERSITY OF CALIFORNIA PRESS
publishes bold, progressive books and journals on topics in the arts, humanities, social sciences, and natural sciences—with a focus on social justice issues—that inspire thought and action among readers worldwide.

The UC PRESS FOUNDATION raises funds to uphold the press's vital role as an independent, nonprofit publisher, and receives philanthropic support from a wide range of individuals and institutions—and from committed readers like you. To learn more, visit ucpress.edu/supportus.

www.ingramcontent.com/pod-product-compliance
Lightning Source LLC
Chambersburg PA
CBHW020542030426

42337CB00013B/947